Management for Professionals

The Springer series "Management for Professionals" comprises high-level business and management books for executives, MBA students, and practice-oriented business researchers. The topics cover all themes relevant to businesses and the business ecosystem. The authors are experienced business professionals and renowned professors who combine scientific backgrounds, best practices, and entrepreneurial vision to provide powerful insights into achieving business excellence.

The Series is SCOPUS-indexed.

Raphael H Cohen

Driving Employee Engagement

A Leader's Guidebook for Peak Performance

 Springer

Raphael H Cohen
Geneva, Switzerland

ISSN 2192-8096 ISSN 2192-810X (electronic)
Management for Professionals
ISBN 978-3-032-05171-4 ISBN 978-3-032-05172-1 (eBook)
https://doi.org/10.1007/978-3-032-05172-1

Translation from the French language edition: "*Les leviers de l'engagement*" by Raphael H Cohen,
© Éditions Eyrolles 2020. Published by Éditions Eyrolles. All Rights Reserved.

This Springer imprint is published by the registered company Springer Nature Switzerland AG.
The registered company address is: Gewerbestrasse 11, 6330 Cham, Switzerland

If disposing of this product, please recycle the paper.

To Ellen, whose caring and love are a constant source of inspiration

Foreword

Last year, I was invited to speak around Brazil for the American Chamber of Commerce's CEO Forum. The theme for 2024 was "Happiness as a Business Strategy." It was bold, and a reminder that something is shifting in the business world.

The CEO Forum draws some of the country's most influential leaders, across every industry. And the fact that *this* was the theme? It speaks volumes about the moment we're in. Because what we're really talking about when we say happiness, is engagement. And engagement, right now, is one of the biggest challenges facing businesses globally.

During my talks, I shared a message that I've been carrying with me for years: that businesses are still operating as if we're in the industrial age; when success meant control, process, and profit above all else. Back then, emotions were irrelevant. People were cogs in the machine.

But that model is broken, and the impact of that outdated thinking is having a significant impact on businesses today.

Trust in business has plummeted. In fact, the Edelman Trust Barometer shows that it's at an all-time low. And when people don't feel seen, supported or understood, they check out. Innovation slows. Absenteeism climbs. People leave. Gallup's 2023 report shows that disengaged employees cost U.S. companies up to $550 billion a year.

And yet, the data are equally clear when you look at things from the other perspective. Engaged teams are 21% more profitable. Happy employees are 400% more innovative. When people are empowered to contribute with heart and purpose, everything changes.

But this shift doesn't come from policies. It comes from people. Specifically, from leaders who understand that the human skills—emotional intelligence, empathy, fairness, care—are no longer optional. What used to be called "soft skills" are now the most strategic levers we have.

That's why this book matters so deeply.

When Raphael H. Cohen first began teaching leadership, he was told, *"We don't have time to be kind, we need to make money."*

Today, he's proving the opposite: If you want profitability, you need engagement. And if you want engagement, you need fairness and kindness.

That's what this book, *Driving Employee Engagement: A Leader's Guidebook for Peak Performance*, delivers. This is not a feel-good ideal, but a practical, evidence-backed, deeply grounded framework for what real leadership looks like today. Leadership that puts people, trust, and meaning at the heart of performance.

Raphael doesn't just talk about the need to care, he shows you how. With precision and clarity, he offers the tools to build teams that thrive not just *for* the organization, but *within* it. Teams that want you as their leader, not because of your title, but because of your trustworthiness. Because you are fair. Because you care.

That's the kind of leadership we need today; the kind that turns bruised apples into preserves and sparks a community movement. That story really got me thinking—it's a powerful reminder that even in the face of setbacks, there's opportunity to adapt, to create meaning, and to serve something greater. Many of the antidotes and stories in the book bring to life how business doesn't have to be a cold machine but can instead be a living, breathing force for collective flourishing.

This isn't easy work. But as Raphael reminds us, it *is* possible. Fair and caring leadership isn't a luxury. It's a necessity. And it's time.

Let this book be your guide.

Founder and CEO, TIE Leadership   Philippa White
Return on Humanity: Leadership Lessons from
All Corners of the World
Olinda, Brazil

Introduction and Warnings

Introduction

This book presents leadership strategies designed to enhance satisfaction for both managers and their teams. It provides practical ideas and tools to develop your skills and refine your leadership style through Fair and Caring Leadership, a style designed to maximize team engagement.

The Fair and Caring leader balances the imperatives of fairness and caring with those of performance, to win the hearts and minds of employees to achieve an agreed-upon cause together.

With over 40 years of experience managing diverse teams across various sectors, including startups, academia, banking, services, and industry, I have been privileged to develop a unique perspective on leadership. I have experienced it from all angles: as a manager, a subordinate, a business school professor teaching executives, a mentor, and through exposure to various managerial situations in companies of all sizes.

These experiences, combined with my learning from field observations, have shaped my understanding of what influences collaborator engagement. This understanding forms the foundation of Fair and Caring Leadership, which I have structured into a practical model and taught for years at leading business schools, large organizations, and small and medium-sized enterprises.[1]

Many participants have confirmed that this approach resonates with their vision, articulates their feelings, and empowers them with practical leadership tools. This positive feedback has motivated me to share Fair and Caring Leadership through this book, aiming to help those who have not had the opportunity to attend my seminars.

This book distills the core principles of Fair and Caring Leadership into a practical operational guide. Rather than a comprehensive treatise, it focuses on essential elements, minimizing quotations and references to provide a clear overview. Although other authors may explore individual topics in greater depth, this book offers a practical foundation by presenting a holistic view of all engagement levers rather than examining each one extensively.

---

[1] Also known as SMEs.

The guiding principle here is common sense, though, as we know, it is not always common practice. Therefore, even fundamental principles merit careful attention, as they are often overlooked in daily operations. The true challenge lies not in understanding these principles but in implementing them consistently. To demonstrate the real-world applicability of Fair and Caring Leadership, authentic but anonymized testimonials are featured throughout the book. After all, leadership manifests in practice, not merely in theory.

I trust that this book will help you avoid the painful and lengthy trial-and-error process that I experienced. More importantly, I hope that implementing Fair and Caring Leadership will bring multiple benefits: enhancing your job satisfaction, improving your team's quality of life at work, boosting performance and agility, and ultimately driving collective success. The good news is that achieving these results requires less effort than you might expect.

This book primarily uses gender-neutral pronouns (such as 'they' for 'he' or 'she'), with occasional traditional masculine forms. This approach maintains my commitment to gender equality while prioritizing readability and inclusivity for all readers.

Warnings

First Warning

This book is based on the principle that work can be a source of satisfaction, gratification, and self-fulfillment. The very etymology of the word "work" supports this view: in German (*Werk*), it shares its root with the Greek word *ergon*, which speaks to human "power" (*dunamis*) and our ability to "put into action." Through this action, humans fulfill themselves. It follows in the footsteps of Douglas McGregor's "Theory Y"[2] and the ancient Greeks, who saw work as a form of freedom.

If you are someone who fundamentally sees work as a burden, this book might not resonate with your current mindset—and that is perfectly okay. This perception reflects the ancient distinction between slave labor (*douleia*) and the creative work of free individuals (*poiein*).[3] Similarly, this book is not intended for devotees of McGregor's Theory X or those who see work merely as a necessary evil—a means of paying bills and putting food on the table. Knowing that only 20% of French people find pleasure in their work,[4] one wonders whether the remaining

---

[2] https://en.wikipedia.org/wiki/Theory_X_and_Theory_Y

[3] As Grégoire Sommer explains: "The modern Greek word for work (*douleia*) recalls the activity of the slave, which was said to be in every way different from the creative work of the free man. For the ancient Greeks, true work was 'poetic' work (from *poiein*: to make, to create), which was the hallmark of the free man, as freedom was defined as that which makes the creative gesture possible. To achieve it, one must have what the slave is deprived of, namely 'leisure' (*scholê*, hence our "school"). In the Christian context, the notion of 'work' is intimately linked to the biblical episode of the fall of man."

[4] As of 2012, the Edenred-Ipsos barometer on employee well-being and motivation (2012).

80% perceive work as *douleia*, or if they find no pleasure in it just because they are poorly managed. In the latter case, this book offers them and their managers the keys to reintroducing pleasure into their daily working lives.

Second Warning

Given the sheer number of levers available to achieve collaborator engagement, it is obvious that being a great leader is no easy task. One of the goals of this book is to highlight this challenge and emphasize the importance of dedicating effort to it. To paraphrase Derek Bok's well-known saying, "If you think education is expensive, try ignorance," I would put it this way: if you find Fair and Caring Leadership costly in terms of time and effort, think about the consequences of bad leadership.

My intention is not to discourage you, but to invite you to be lucid about the levers required to become a great leader and mindful of the consequences of ignoring them. Mastering all the levers is probably unrealistic. You must therefore strive to do your best with each of these levers, while remaining aware that perfection is beyond anyone's reach. Employees accept their leader's imperfections if they are convinced that they are sincerely trying to do what is best for their team.

Making good soup does not take any longer or cost more than making a bad one. The difference lies in whether someone has made the prior effort to learn how to cook and invest the time in assimilating best practices. Those who start preparing meals without first understanding the basics will eventually pay the price for their lack of knowledge. The same applies to leadership: just as a good cook loves good food, a good leader must genuinely care about people and be invested in their well-being.

This implies that not everyone is cut out to be a true leader. Anyone with the ambition to lead must accept that it is a responsibility—one that requires the effort to understand the levers of engagement and the willingness to devote time and attention to others.

The easy way to get others to do what you want is to use force or exercise hierarchical authority. The disadvantage is that your employees will do the bare minimum to avoid losing their jobs. To prevent this, you need to be prepared to devote time and attention to your employees. This book is for those who are not only willing to make that investment and reap its rewards, but who are able to make room in their schedule for others.

For those who feel that they do not have the time to apply these principles, there are enough books on time management for me to refrain from explaining their recommendations here! I believe that we always find time for what is important to us. I remember, for example, an executive who said he did not have time for sports, but who completely changed his tune after suffering a cardiac incident. When his cardiologist explained that if he did not exercise, his next appointment would be at the cemetery, he was shocked and miraculously found time to work out. It all comes down to priorities.

The good news is that the initial investment in learning Fair and Caring Leadership, along with the efforts required to implement it, results in performance and a level of gratification far superior to approaches based on the exercise of power centered on hierarchical authority.

Acknowledgments

This is not an encyclopedic presentation proving that I have read a hundred books and now written the 101st incorporating all previous knowledge. I humbly acknowledge that I could not have discovered all the information in this book by myself—I do not live in a vacuum. Over my 40-plus years as an entrepreneur and intrapreneur, I have read many books and articles, attended countless training seminars and lectures, and worked with numerous people on real business opportunities in real time.

This combined experience taught me many things, but I never took the time to note their sources. The content of this book integrates what I have learned from all these experiences. I must apologize to academics, professors, writers, consultants, and gurus when I have not acknowledged the source of concepts that they developed. I have no plagiaristic intention to steal their ideas—just the limited memory of a recent entrepreneurship professor who never thought he would be writing books. When I was simply a businessman, I had not even considered becoming a public speaker, lecturer, professor, or writer.

Because trying to identify all sources would be too time-consuming and as with this book I have no academic ambition, I decided to publish it with only those academic sources, quotes, and references that I could remember. I welcome any information that will allow me to give proper credit where it is due. I will be grateful to anyone who writes to me at author@driving-engagement.com, indicating who should receive credit and for what. I will update future editions with all the sources, quotes, and references I receive.

I am particularly thankful to all the people I have worked with who helped me to learn what employees need and want. I have made many mistakes as a leader, and thanks to their benevolent and forgiving support, I have little by little learned to become a less bad leader. Leading is a constant work in progress.

I would also like to thank everyone who participated in my leadership-training sessions. Their challenging questions helped me to further improve the Fair and Caring Leadership toolbox and progressively develop it to its current level.

I am very grateful to my wife, Ellen, and my children, who have been so understanding, despite my lack of presence and availability while working on this book. The connection between business concepts and humor was certainly inspired by the many jokes my father told me to illustrate business situations. The messages he conveyed were not only fun but also easy to remember.

As this book was originally written in French and English is not my mother tongue, I asked the artificial intelligence tool Claude to help me translate from French to English. Besides the quality of the translation, I have been impressed by the spontaneous suggestions and relevant comments that Claude made. I am therefore very grateful to Claude for being such a useful sparring partner.

Special thanks also go to Ellen for fine-tuning the result of my interaction with Claude, suggesting several improvements and acting as an excellent sounding board and advisor.

Competing Interests   The author is a co-founder and co-owner of EazyMirror, a tool referenced in this book. The author is also managing MicroMBA programs, executive education programs mentioned in this book.

Contents

List of Levers

A Few Basics

1.1 The Problem and the Approach

When studies[1] reveal that 65% of employees would prefer to change their manager rather than receive a pay rise, or that 26% of Canadians would prefer their manager to be a robot,[2] it becomes evident that significant problems exist in team management. The employee distress I observe in the vast majority of companies demonstrates that traditional management methods are no longer effective enough to meet today's workplace demands.[3]

This observation gave birth to this book, inviting you to reflect on your own approaches to leadership. Although it does not attempt to address every leadership issue comprehensively, it presents an impressionistic picture that interconnects various parameters, encouraging you to step back and discover your own truth. Indeed, there is not just one leadership style but several, each effective under different circumstances.

Rather than relying solely on academic studies that typically focus on limited parameters, I have taken a holistic approach that is more empirical and pragmatic than academic. Although I occasionally reference scholarly work, the content of this book is grounded in my personal leadership experience across various roles, combined with observations from numerous companies where I teach and from which my MBA students come. The meaningful exchanges with course

"Introduction and Warnings" for this book are available in Front matter and "Epilogue" and "Complete Framework for Building Trust, High Engagement, and High Performance" are available in Back matter. Readers can download them free from https://doi.org/10.1007/978-3-032-05172-1.

[1] www.inc.com/maeghan-ouimet/real-cost-bad-bosses.html

[2] https://www.intensions.co/news/2016/3/29/intensions-future-of-work

[3] Another example: https://www.swissinfo.ch/fre/societe/malades-du-stress_la-souffrance-au-travail%2D%2Dtoujours-un-tabou/32549108

© The Author(s), under exclusive license to Springer Nature
Switzerland AG 2026
R. H Cohen, *Driving Employee Engagement*, Management for Professionals,
https://doi.org/10.1007/978-3-032-05172-1_1

participants have provided an extraordinary source of insight—their questions and examples have significantly shaped this work.

1.2   Are You Trustworthy?

"As trust is the basis of all forms of influence other than coercion,"[4] you, as a manager, must inevitably examine what parameters influence the level of trust your colleagues place in you. This becomes even more critical as trust in superiors directly correlates with the achievement of objectives.

As Kouzes and Posner[5] astutely observe, "If you don't believe in the messenger, you won't believe the message." Without trust, your words will not resonate with your colleagues. Without resorting to force, it would be entirely illusory to believe that you can influence someone who does not trust you.

In the professional world, force manifests through two Levers, both fundamentally based on mechanisms of constraint:

- Money, which serves as both carrot and stick: remuneration depends on submission to authority
- The power conferred by hierarchical position: the authority to punish noncompliance and reward compliance

By choosing either of these levers, you exercise power in a discretionary manner, which generates insecurity and fear among your employees.

Fortunately, there exists a third lever that does not require force: inspiring your employees to engage willingly, transforming them into engaged individuals. However, earning their engagement requires their trust.

My empirical research and experience indicate that employee trust depends on four key factors:

- Your adherence to agreed specific values and imperatives
- Their acceptance of your governance arrangements and how this governance is experienced and enforced
- The alignment between your behavior and the behavior they expect from you
- Your personal qualities and character traits

To help you understand and remember these trust-influencing parameters, these four broad categories form the columns of the Complete Framework for Building Trust, High Engagement, and High Performance presented at the end of this book (also available for download at www.driving-engagement.com/download). Each column details the elements that determine your employees' trust levels. These levers inevitably determine their level of engagement.

---

[4] Hurley RF (2011) The decision to trust. Harv Bus Rev 89(1/2):114–123.

[5] James Kouzes and Barry Posner, "If you don't believe the messenger, you won't believe the message", in The Leadership Challenge, John Wiley & Sons, 2017.

Given the numerous parameters listed, establishing trustworthiness presents a significant challenge.

In Practice

Being aware that your colleagues evaluate you continuously based on these parameters requires constant vigilance. If maintaining this level of awareness and consistency feels beyond your capabilities, sustaining a leadership role in the long term will prove challenging.

The summary table reveals a crucial insight: your colleagues interpret all your actions through the lens of their accumulated trust in you. The greater their trust, the more understanding they will be of your inevitable mistakes (inevitable because perfection remains unattainable). Conversely, when trust is low, even minor missteps face harsh judgment. Therefore, from a strategic perspective, continuously nurturing and developing trust provides an essential buffer for those inevitable moments when you need it.

However, be mindful that approaching trust building as merely a tactical tool will ultimately fail. Employees readily discern when benevolence or caring is not genuine. To maintain authentic trust, genuine care for your employees' well-being must form the foundation of your leadership approach.

1.3   What Level of Engagement Do You Get?

1.3.1   Economic Impact of Engaged Employees

Employee engagement manifests through their desire to contribute to organizational success, their willingness to become involved, their investment, and their level of psychological ownership.[6] Anyone who doubts its importance is living in a fantasy world.

Let me be brutally honest about the numbers: PricewaterhouseCoopers' research stated that engaged employees skyrocket productivity and profits by up to 35%.[7] This is not mere theory. Gretchen Spreitzer and Christine Porath[8] hammer home this reality—satisfied employees crush productivity targets, remain loyal, and go above and beyond expectations. Even more damning, they expose how workplace incivility acts like a virus, poisoning performance as victims spread their frustrations through the organization like a toxic plague.

As engagement levels make or break performance, not measuring them is organizational malpractice. A team delivering "acceptable" results while disengaged is like an athlete competing at half strength—it is a waste of potential that

---

[6] https://en.wikipedia.org/wiki/Ownership_(psychology)

[7] Global Human Capital Survey, PwC, March 2003; corroborated by recent Gallup studies.

[8] Gretchen Spreitzer and Christine Porath, "Creating Sustainable Performance," Harvard Business Review, January–February 2012.

should infuriate any serious leader and all shareholders. (The nuts and bolts of measuring engagement follow in the next sections.)

Given the demonstrable economic impact of engagement levels, failing to measure them should be a criminal offense. Some may avoid measurement to escape confronting an uncomfortable reality: their failure to fulfill their mission of fostering engagement. Managers who fear measuring their team's engagement levels often display remarkable creativity in undermining such measurements and the effort to implement them. Their concern about the side effects of the measurement, including the impact of potentially poor scores, overshadows a fundamental truth: for collective success, having measurement data—even if it reveals deficiencies—proves more valuable than having no data at all.

Those who function merely as managers, rather than as leaders, show little concern for maximizing their team's potential and the organization's overall success. They privilege protecting their job. This raises a critical question: should protecting the career of an ineffective manager or ensuring collective success that sustains the organization in the long term take precedence?

Let us call it what it is: managers confident in their leadership skills welcome engagement measurement with open arms. Those who fight against it are essentially confessing their incompetence. There is no middle ground here: you either measure and improve, or you hide and fail. The choice speaks volumes about your fitness to lead.

1.3.2 Forms of Engagement

To be blunt, employee engagement is not merely about workplace happiness—it is the cornerstone of organizational survival. Let us be crystal clear: this is not some feel-good HR concept—it is the lifeblood of organizational performance and sustainability. As a leader, your primary mission—your absolute imperative—is to maximize the engagement of every employee for whom you are responsible. This means igniting their passion to excel, compelling them to pour their energy into the collective mission.

Engagement is not a one-size-fits-all concept. It manifests in four distinct forms, each with profound implications:

- Personal Drive Engagement: raw, intrinsic motivation in its purest form. This is the fundamental desire to achieve, regardless of its source. It is the baseline of human ambition.
- Individual Success Engagement: the realm of personal ambition and self-interest. This is also the default setting of mediocre management—relying on crude carrots and sticks to drive individual achievement through personal targets. It breeds a toxic "every-person-for-themselves" culture, where individual bonuses reign supreme and collective success becomes collateral damage.
- Engagement for the Cause: the power of purpose in action. When people connect deeply with organizational intent, they become unstoppable. Such is its power that it can sustain engagement even under subpar leadership—although this is hardly ideal.

- Collective Success Engagement: the ultimate leadership achievement—where team synergy creates extraordinary results that dwarf individual accomplishments. Although it still celebrates personal contributions, it demands that everyone elevates their game for collective triumph. Regrettably, most development programs completely miss this, obsessing over individual competencies while failing to grasp the art of collective excellence. Creating a winning team requires far more than empty platitudes about teamwork in mission statements.

Here is the unvarnished truth: too many managers lazily default to encouraging individual success when true leadership excellence demands mastering collective success engagement. Your mission is not to breed an army of self-serving achievers—it is to forge an unstoppable "we" that demolishes collective goals.

This leads us to the definitive test of leadership: your ability to ignite passionate engagement for collective success through genuine teamwide collaboration. This ability should be measured. The metrics do not lie—they expose your real impact as a leader. Whether engagement comes through autocratic leadership or a completely different style is irrelevant—what matters is that it works in your context.

Results trump style in achieving engagement, provided you operate within ethical boundaries and organizational guidelines. Although the ends cannot justify all means, and organizations must establish non-negotiable principles, that framework discussion awaits another day. What matters now is ensuring that your governance respects these fundamentals. Consider this a given—the complete roadmap for implementation will be detailed in my next book.

Lever 24 • Have Engaged Followers

Let me demolish a persistent myth: there is no single "correct" leadership style.[9] **Measuring engagement levels liberates us from the tyranny of leadership prescriptions and the endless debate about which approach reigns supreme**. If there were a universal formula for leadership excellence, we would have discovered it by now, and libraries would not be groaning under the weight of countless leadership theories.

The beauty of measuring results is its brutal honesty—it cuts through the noise of methodology debates and theoretical posturing. When you have hard data on engagement levels as an outcome, the "how" becomes secondary to the "what." If your team is fully engaged and crushing objectives, who are we to dictate your leadership style? Conversely, if engagement is tanking, that is your wake-up call to rethink your approach.

Here is the undeniable truth: although leadership styles may be debatable, the necessity of achieving employee engagement is not. It is the one non-negotiable outcome that separates exceptional leaders from mediocre managers.

---

[9] The number in the left margin corresponds to the lever number in the comprehensive Framework for Building Trust, High Engagement, and High Performance at the end of this book.

This is precisely why measuring engagement trumps philosophizing about methods—results speak louder than theories.

The Four Critical Questions That Expose True Leadership

1. Is your team crushing its mission and objectives? This demands crystal-clear, measurable targets—and not a sprawling wish list. (We will dive deep into this in Chap. 5.)
2. Are you extracting maximum collective engagement from your team? Bluntly put: are they operating at peak potential, or are you leaving performance on the table?
3. Do your people want you as their leader?[10] This is the acid test: can you lead without wielding the hammer of hierarchical authority? Your team's trust in you tells the real story. Let us be brutally honest—if you must remind people of your title to get things done, you have failed as a leader. Without willing followers, you are merely a manager with a fancy title.
4. Based on your team's feedback, what additional steps must you still take to obtain peak engagement?

These four questions, when combined, create an unforgiving mirror that exposes the truth about your leadership. Taking them individually risks self-deception; together, they leave nowhere to hide.

The first two questions determine whether you are delivering the goods. Your own leadership credibility in the organization lives or dies by these metrics. After all, like any employee, you must perform—but with the added responsibility of maximizing team engagement. If you cannot do this, what exactly is the point of your management role?

The third question cuts to the heart of authentic leadership: do you have genuinely engaged followers? Leadership demands voluntary followers—people who choose to follow you, not because they must, but because they want to. This is the essence of true leadership, provided that it stems from trust and inspiration, not from fear or coercion. Measuring this willingness to follow is non-negotiable, as it directly correlates with trust levels. Without trust, you have compliance, not engagement.

The fourth question provides your roadmap for improvement, targeting enhanced engagement and trust—the twin pillars of effective leadership. These elements form the backbone of this book and the core of Fair and Caring Leadership. Like the North Star, they must guide every leadership decision you make.

---

[10] Robert Goffee and Gareth Jones, "Why Should Anyone Be Led by You? What It Takes To Be An Authentic Leader," Harvard Business Review Press, 2006.

The Parable of the Productive Ant

Once there was a remarkably productive Ant who bounded into work early each day. She worked with genuine joy, even singing while delivering outstanding results. Her only "flaw"? She had no manager...

The CEO, a pompous Hornet, found this situation utterly unacceptable. "Unmanaged productivity? Impossible!" He promptly created a management position, recruiting an "experienced" Beetle. The Beetle's first "crucial" task? Implementing rigid time-tracking systems. Soon came the avalanche of reports and forms. This "essential" bureaucracy demanded a secretary, so in came a Spider, armed with filing systems and telephone protocols.

Meanwhile, the Ant kept doing what she did best: delivering results.

The Hornet, intoxicated by the Beetle's endless reports, demanded more— comparative studies, graphs, trend analyses, and performance indicators. Enter the Cockroach, a "management assistant," complete with new computer systems and printers.

Predictably, the once-joyful Ant began drowning in paperwork, her productivity suffocating under the weight of administrative demands.

Sensing a "management opportunity," the Hornet created a department manager position. Enter the Cicada, who immediately required premium office furniture, an ergonomic throne, and cutting-edge technology. Of course, this necessitated a network server. And naturally, the Cicada needed a deputy (conveniently, an old colleague) to craft "strategic management plans" and departmental budgets.

The Ant's joy and productivity continued their death spiral.

"We need a workplace climate study, " declared the Cicada, blind to the obvious.

Finally, the Hornet examined the financial results and discovered— shock!—that the department's profitability had plummeted. His solution? Hire an expensive consultant, the "distinguished" Owl.

After three months of "intensive analysis" (and substantial fees), the Owl delivered his profound insight: "This department is overstaffed."

The Hornet's response? He fired the Ant.

Source: Anonymous, but painfully true in many organizations.

1.3.3   How to Measure the Level of Engagement That You Generate

Although the preceding questions serve your personal leadership reflection, measuring your team's actual engagement is not optional—it is imperative. Yet here lies a critical distinction: most so-called engagement surveys conducted in organizations are merely climate assessments. They measure collective commitment to the organization or its mission, and sometimes they gauge intrinsic motivation. However, they rarely measure what truly matters—the genuine level of engagement that each leader obtains from their teams.

When these surveys do attempt to measure leadership-driven engagement, they stumble into two devastating pitfalls:

- **The Indirect Measurement Fallacy**: instead of measuring engagement directly, these surveys obsess over proxy behaviors that supposedly indicate engagement. They bombard employees with questions such as "Does your boss give you enough autonomy?" or "Does your manager value your opinion?" and then deduce engagement levels from these behaviors. This is as relevant as relying on the ingredient list to guess the taste of the final dish.

  This approach arrogantly assumes that there is one universal recipe for engagement—a dangerously flawed premise. Because the complex leadership–engagement relationship defies such simplistic formulas, reality demolishes this assumption: a manager can check all the behavioral boxes but still fail to generate engagement, or vice versa.

- **The Fear Factor**: employees often lie in these surveys. Why? Because they know that both HR and their boss will dissect every response with surgical precision. Despite promises of anonymity (which many employees doubt), fear of retaliation forces them to sanitize their responses. The result? Data that are worse than useless—they are misleading.

In Practice

This observation leads me to recommend an alternative approach to measuring engagement scores: the Management-Generated Engagement Score (MGES).[11] It is a more direct, powerful method for assessing true leadership effectiveness.

Instead of relying on indirect deductions, the MGES measures engagement as an outcome of all managerial practices through direct, unambiguous questions. Here are some examples of core questions, rated on a scale of 0–4:

1. How likely are you to recommend a friend to join the team led by your direct manager?
2. How much does your direct manager inspire you to give your best performance?
3. How strongly do you want to continue working under your direct manager's leadership?
4. How effective is your direct manager at attracting and retaining high-performing team members?

---

[11] Although various tools meet these requirements, www.EazyMirror.com/MGES offers a free measurement of the "Management-Generated Engagement Score (MGES)," making this methodology accessible to all while fully protecting respondents' anonymity.

To ensure honest responses, absolute anonymity and confidentiality must be guaranteed—not just promised.

For putting managers in control, I recommend implementing a two-phase reporting system that leverages EazyMirror's features:

- **Phase 1**: Initial scores, along with the average score of other managers in the organization, are transmitted exclusively to each manager in a strictly confidential manner. Managers retain complete autonomy over if, when, and with whom to share their scores. This ensures psychological safety conducive to self-reflection and improvement.
- **Phase 2**: After a predetermined grace period, their subsequent scores become accessible to predefined stakeholders (superiors, HR, or peers). Managers know that they will be held accountable when their MGES is shared, but that they have the grace period to improve their score.

This grace period serves a vital purpose: it gives managers time to enhance their leadership capabilities through training or alternative approaches while empowering them to take control of their leadership journey. Experience shows that this often motivates those with lower scores to actively seek professional development.

Most critically, this measurement system reveals whether a manager is indeed maximizing their team's potential performance. It answers the fundamental question: Is the team's current performance merely adequate, despite low engagement, or does it represent the best possible outcome because the leader has successfully maximized their team's engagement?

As the MGES only measures the actual outcome, it avoids assumptions about causality by measuring only the result: the real level of manager-generated engagement.

The key difference between traditional surveys and the MGES is that traditional surveys diagnose what managers do, the MGES measures what managers achieve. Leadership should focus only on outcomes and let each manager be responsible for diagnosing their ability to generate that outcome and act accordingly.

When managers can see both their performance results and the engagement behind those results, they can take action to improve the level of engagement that they generate to unlock their team's full potential.

1.4   Enhancing Key Performance Indicator-Focused Management Assessment

Traditional management assessment through key performance indicators (KPIs) and deliverables provides valuable performance data, but ignores a critical parameter: What is the engagement level of those delivering this

performance? The KPIs tell you what was achieved, but do not empower managers to understand whether their teams are performing at their true potential.

This absence of qualification of the performance level achieved leaves managers without the actionable insights that they need to improve. A team can consistently meet KPI targets with disengaged employees, but managers may not realize the tremendous untapped potential on the table. When managers have access to the engagement they generate alongside performance metrics, they can take ownership of maximizing their teams' capabilities.

The MGES introduced earlier provides managers with the actionable insight they need: concrete data on the engagement outcomes that they actually achieve with their teams.

The MGES empowers managers by complementing traditional KPI reviews with feedback on the engagement outcomes that they generate. Although KPIs show what was delivered, the MGES reveals whether managers are creating the conditions in which their teams can excel. This puts the power—and responsibility—directly in managers' hands to explore and activate potential improvements.

1.5   Leveraging Engagement to Attract Top Talent

A strong engagement score becomes a powerful magnet for exceptional talent. When candidates know that their potential manager consistently inspires high team engagement and genuine enthusiasm, they actively seek to join that team. After all, top performers recognize the value of working under a leader who demonstrably maximizes team potential and cultivates meaningful engagement. This creates a virtuous cycle—high engagement scores attract premier talent, which in turn contributes to even stronger team performance.

In Practice

I recommend that every job candidate poses two key questions during their interview:

1. "Does your organization measure manager-driven team engagement?"

   This question reveals volumes about organizational priorities. When an organization chooses not to measure engagement, it signals how little they value employee perspective. Remember: what isn't measured is not valued.

2. "What is my potential manager's MGES (Management-Generated Engagement Score)?"

   The answer—or lack thereof—speaks directly to your future work experience. A strong score predicts a positive environment; a poor score or reluctance to share this information serves as a warning signal.

These questions accomplish far more than gathering information—they provide insight into organizational culture that proves far more valuable than carefully crafted employer branding. They expose the true DNA of the company: its commitment to leadership quality and employee experience.

Moreover, as more candidates demand this transparency, organizations will face increasing pressure to ensure that their managers excel at engaging their teams. This creates a powerful incentive for positive change—one interview at a time.

1.6   Dual Accountability: A Leadership Imperative

The traditional model of upward-only accountability has created a dangerous imbalance in organizational dynamics. When managers focus exclusively on pleasing their superiors, who often accept surface-level success without examining team engagement, they create a fundamentally flawed leadership approach.

This one-sided accountability breeds a toxic "minimum viable effort" mentality. Managers learn that they need only to prevent outright rebellion or mass exodus, rather than cultivating genuine engagement. This creates a perverse incentive to extract maximum output while investing minimal resources in team well-being—the "squeeze-the-lemon" approach that rewards those who flatter upward while oppressing downward.

However, this destructive pattern is not inevitable. When you recognize that a manager's primary mission is maximizing team engagement, the path forward becomes clear: leaders must be equally as accountable to their teams as to their superiors. It is unthinkable that team members would fully engage when they sense that their leader does not genuinely care about their well-being.

True leadership requires symmetrical accountability—demonstrating equal respect for both superiors and team members. This accountability requires earning trust through fair treatment and genuine care—creating an environment where team members naturally choose to give their best. This dual responsibility is particularly important for younger generations, who reject authority based solely on hierarchical position and demand genuine consideration.

This balance is not merely an ethical choice; it is a strategic imperative for achieving sustainable high performance. Leaders must embrace this dual responsibility, recognizing that fairness and care are not optional luxuries but essential components of effective leadership.

1.7   Different Paths to Lasting Engagement

Employee preferences in leadership styles vary dramatically. Some thrive under direct instruction, whereas others require participative management. Certain team members seek decision-making involvement, whereas others prefer to let management decide. Work-style preferences range from strict adherence to business hours to flexible overtime, from proactive initiative-taking to careful task execution.

Given this diversity, no single management style fits all. There is therefore no magic one-size-fits-all formula to generate engagement. Success hinges on achieving the right match between employees and their manager—a relationship that works both ways. The key is measuring whether the manager maximizes team engagement while protecting their psychological and physical well-being, focusing on outcomes rather than methods.

Indeed, measuring team engagement levels remains the only reliable way of determining if a leadership approach optimizes outcomes.

However, it is crucial to ensure that engagement is lasting. Some experts, despite being poor leaders, still attract young people eager to learn. These employees invest time to acquire experience before fleeing. Consider young people who accept working seven days a week in investment banking or consulting firms, hoping to eventually succeed. This represents submission disguised as engagement—a toxic prerequisite for success in some corporate cultures, not genuine lasting engagement.

1.8 The Big Engagement Picture and Its Impact on Performance

As managers are not the only ones responsible for engagement levels, shareholders and leadership should also measure the engagement generated by the organization. This separation allows each party accountability for their specific sphere: managers for their behavior and decisions, top management for work conditions, compensation, HR policies, and company image.

When this separation blurs, accountability diminishes. When responsibility is unclear, each party blames the other, and nobody remains truly accountable.

Many organizations believe that they already measure engagement through satisfaction or climate surveys. As explained above[12] these traditional satisfaction surveys only reveal part of the story.

However, what matters is whether your organization generates enough appreciation that employees recommend it and demonstrate daily engagement. An organization can have "satisfied" employees who neither recommend the company nor want to give their best. Appreciation goes far beyond satisfaction: It reveals whether teams are true organizational ambassadors.

---

[12] See Sect. 1.3.3.

In Practice

I recommend using the Employee Appreciation Score (EAS), which measures two concrete outcomes: how well your organization and managers succeed in generating appreciation and engagement from your employees.

Unlike traditional approaches that attempt to explain through diagnosis without necessarily measuring the desired outcome, the EAS reveals your ability to create an environment where your teams want to give the best of themselves.

The four questions measured by the EAS are:

1. How likely are you to recommend your employer to a friend who is considering working there?
2. How much do your employer's framework conditions and strategy motivate you to give your best?
3. How likely are you to recommend your direct manager to a friend who is considering joining their team?
4. How much does your direct manager make you want to give your best?

EazyMirror[13] proposes two options:

- The Standard EAS: Using the reference survey questions of its inter-company barometer that allows benchmarking your organization with the average of other participating organizations
- The Customized EAS: Customizing the questions according to your specific needs for a tailor-made measurement (without a benchmark)

---

[13] www.EazyMirror.com/EAS provides a freemium version with specific features that ensure respondents' psychological safety.

Sustainability, Fairness and Caring: Three Essential Imperatives

2

2.1 The Question of Values

When it comes to making decisions and guiding your choices, you need points of reference. Values are one of them, but they are rarely explicit enough in organizations. Most organizational "values" are merely expected behaviors, not true values. In the professional world, the notion of value and its manifestations are so overused that the question is often reduced to a cosmetic exercise.

What is worse is that announced values rarely translate into lived experience. The most telling evidence for this disconnect is that employees seldom remember their organization's stated values. If these values were genuine and enforceable, employees would know them by heart and actively demand their respect.

The distinction between values and expected behaviors often remains unclear owing to imprecise definitions. Having personally struggled to explain what a value is—and finding none of the existing definitions fully satisfactory—I offer this synthesis based on key insights from colleagues.[1]

A value is something a person upholds for its own sake, not as a means of achieving something else. Although people may differ in what they consider fundamentally important, for each individual, their core values are clear and non-negotiable principles that guide their decisions and actions.

Values serve as direct guides for our actions and reactions when we act in their name. When you can say "I do this in the name of X," X is likely to be a value.

"Introduction and Warnings" for this book are available in Front matter and "Epilogue" and "Complete Framework for Building Trust, High Engagement, and High Performance" are available in Back matter. Readers can download them free from https://doi.org/10.1007/978-3-032-05172-1.

---

[1] Notably Professors Yves Semen and Guido Palazzo.

© The Author(s), under exclusive license to Springer Nature Switzerland AG 2026
R. H Cohen, *Driving Employee Engagement*, Management for Professionals, https://doi.org/10.1007/978-3-032-05172-1_2

For instance, when you refuse favoritism by stating "I do this in the name of fairness," you are invoking fairness as a core value.

True values are principles you are ready to defend and fight for. The depth of your commitment to a value manifests in your willingness to stand up for it, even in challenging circumstances.

In professional settings, values should create both obligations and rights that every employee can invoke, regardless of their position within the organization. When a principle only creates obligations without conferring corresponding rights, you should consider whether it has been reduced to merely expected behavior rather than standing as a true value.

These criteria, although neither perfect nor exhaustive, offer pragmatic guidance for professional settings. Rather than attempting to provide a comprehensive definition, they serve as practical tools for everyday use in the workplace. In this book, a value is defined as a principle upheld for its own sake, in the name of which an individual takes specific actions, feeling morally compelled to do so rather than seeing it as a choice.

Values, contrary to popular belief, are not universal. Although I hold life and family well-being as fundamental values, some parents indoctrinate their young children, who are too young to make independent decisions to become human bombs against perceived enemies. This stark example demonstrates how individuals can operate from radically different value systems.

Values are inherently personal, though shared values create natural communities and facilitate collective living. Coexisting with people whose core values differ significantly from your own can be particularly challenging. Consider, for instance, a partnership where one person values money above all else—to the point of sacrificing relationships for financial gain—whereas the other prioritizes benevolence. Such partners will likely face constant conflict when decisions involve spending money on employee well-being, as they lack the common value foundation necessary to reach meaningful compromise.

Sharing values within a community does not guarantee identical approaches to moral dilemmas. As dilemmas inherently arise from conflicts between values, their resolution depends on how individuals prioritize competing values. Romeo and Juliet's classic dilemma illustrates this perfectly: their tragic choice to prioritize love over family loyalty demonstrates how personal value hierarchies ultimately shape our decisions, even when facing devastating consequences.

Group members must align not only on shared values but also on their hierarchical order to guide interactions and decisions effectively. Establishing value priorities in advance, during periods of calm and objectivity, can prevent numerous conflicts and misunderstandings. When you discuss value rankings without immediate stakes or pressure, you create space for thoughtful reflection and genuine agreement. Conversely, attempting to establish priorities during emotionally charged situations or when immediate interests are at stake tends to cloud judgment and impede rational discussion.

Owing to frequent misunderstandings around the word "value," I deliberately avoid using it in governance documents, opting instead for "imperatives."

This term more effectively conveys the non-negotiable nature of these principles—everyone must respect them, without exception. These imperatives form the essential framework that protects and sustains the group.

Throughout years of leadership experience, I have reached a personal conclusion about earning team trust: it requires honoring three essential imperatives in a specific order. These non-negotiable principles are:

1. Collective success for sustainability
2. Fairness (and equity)
3. Caring or Benevolence

Although you may incorporate additional imperatives into your leadership approach, failing to uphold any one of these three core principles will severely limit your ability to build genuine trust and foster optimal team engagement. The significance of these imperatives cannot be overstated—they form the foundation for every concept and practice presented in this book.

Without full commitment to all three, the methods and approaches that follow will most likely prove less effective.

2.2   Sustainability and Its Corollary: Collective Success

Like living organisms, organizations possess an inherent survival instinct and will swiftly—sometimes excessively—counter any perceived threat to their existence. Expecting an organization to remain passive in the face of danger is unrealistic. It will invariably react, even if this means taking actions that deviate from its normal principles.

When a company shuts down an underperforming production unit, it does so in the name of long-term survival. You might question whether closing a specific facility genuinely serves the company's long-term viability, but you cannot dispute the underlying intention of ensuring survival. The issue at hand is not the goal of sustainability itself, but rather the appropriateness of the methods chosen to achieve it.

The most effective path to organizational longevity lies in maximizing the collective success of all employees. Since sustainability and its corollary, collective success, exist as principles upheld for their own sake, they constitute an imperative that binds every employee. Success and sustainability inherently demand performance—the higher a team's performance, the greater its chances of enduring. Performance, therefore, stands as an essential prerequisite for sustainability.

I propose placing sustainability, coupled with collective performance and success, at the apex of our imperative hierarchy of organizations.

As a manager, delivering collective performance is not just your job—it is your fundamental obligation. If you fail to meet this requirement, the organization will likely determine that you are no longer needed, and you will find yourself facing dismissal. Whether you are the CEO protecting your shareholders' investment or a manager at any other level, you cannot escape this fundamental obligation to drive collective performance that ensures organizational longevity.

2.3   Fairness, the Cornerstone of Trust and Safety

Both equity and fairness strive to achieve what is right and just. This requires carefully weighing competing interests in decision-making. What is right or just, like justice itself, is not absolute but fundamentally a matter of perception. People who share the same worldview are more naturally inclined to share a common understanding of what is "right" and "just."

You must not confuse fairness (as well as equity) with equality, which merely demands identical treatment regardless of circumstances. Building on Aristotle's principles outlined in his *Politics*, some argue that "the worst form of inequality is to try to make unequal things equal."

The centrality of fairness in this framework stems from its direct connection to a fundamental human need. Empirical evidence shows that the perception of unfairness—commonly experienced as a sense of injustice—is what drives people to disengage or even go ballistic. This occurs when promises are broken or when power is wielded to benefit some at the expense of others.

Each instance of power abuse not only exposes the vulnerability of its victims but also suggests the possibility of future transgressions. The direct consequence is a pervasive sense of insecurity affecting everyone except those wielding discretionary power. Consider how unsafe you would feel in a country where laws were routinely ignored. Although this represents an extreme scenario, it effectively illustrates the vital link between fairness and psychological safety.

2.3.1   Fairness and Safety

The importance of security in human psychology is evident from its position in Maslow's hierarchy, appearing immediately after physiological needs. Security, both physical and psychological, plays a vital role in human behavior. Given that fear ranks among the most powerful driving forces in all living beings, the imperative nature of safety becomes clear.

Our survival instinct continuously scans for potential threats, and unfairness—which signals unpredictable decision-making—serves as a warning of future dangers. This perhaps explains children's acute sensitivity to unfairness ("my brother got a bigger piece of cake..."). By instinctively demanding fairness, they protect themselves against future threats. When even animals demonstrate sensitivity to unfairness,[2] it is no surprise that humans react so strongly against it.

---

[2] See for instance Sarah F. Brosnan and Frans B. M. de Waal, "Review: Evolution of responses to (un)fairness," Sciences, 2014, vol. 346, n° 6207.

The concept of psychological security lies at the heart of "Care to Dare: Unleashing Astonishing Potential through Secure Base Leadership"[3] by George Kohlrieser, Susan Goldsworthy, and Duncan Coombe—a book I strongly recommend. Their managerial approaches align perfectly with the principles presented in this book.

As unfairness directly undermines psychological safety, you have no choice but to be fair if you want your employees to feel secure and to... trust you.

2.3.2   Fairness Is Essential for Trust

The question of equity emerges whenever resources must be shared, as distribution inherently requires criteria that demand fairness. Equity involves carefully weighing various interests to determine appropriate allocations for each party. Problems arise when someone perceives that distribution criteria, although claimed to be fair, appear unjust in practice.

This tension manifests in numerous workplace scenarios. Consider the fundamental debate over profit distribution between shareholders and workers, or the employee who questions receiving a smaller bonus than a colleague. These examples underscore how distribution criteria lie at the very heart of fairness discussions.

What employee would trust someone who is not fair? The answer is self-evident—fairness is just as essential for building trust as creating a sense of security.

2.3.3   The Price of Unfairness

The perception of unfairness ignites a deep-seated anger in people. The resulting irritation, frustration, or outright anger can inflict considerable damage, potentially threatening an organization's survival.

Disregarding fairness carries a hefty cost. It inevitably leads to disengagement—it would be delusional to expect an employee to remain engaged when facing unfair treatment from superiors. The consequences extend beyond mere disengagement to include rule-breaking behaviors, ranging from sabotage to economic crimes.

Given that a lack of fairness obviously poses a significant risk, I find it puzzling that organizations do not take it more seriously. Although enforcing fairness within organizations may appear idealistic, experience demonstrates that it is entirely achievable.[4]

---

[3] George Kohlrieser, Susan Goldsworthy and Duncan Coombe, "Care to Dare: Unleashing astonishing potential through secure base leadership," Warren Bennis Books, 2012.
[4] See my article "La justice, talon d'Achille des organisations," Expansion Management Review, September 2010.

2.4   Caring

Would you want to follow a manager who does not care about his employees? In other words, can you trust someone who does not care about your well-being? This question gets the same answer as the one about who would want to follow a leader who is not perceived as fair.

To cultivate engaged followers—particularly those who are intelligent and discerning—a leader must demonstrate not only fairness but also genuine caring toward them.

2.4.1   What Is Caring?

Caring means genuinely accepting and respecting others while actively supporting their interests[5]—a concept distinctly different from mere kindness, which is about pleasing others. To avoid confusion, caring involves thoughtful consideration of what serves someone's well-being, rather than just trying to please them.

> **Case Study: The Cost of Misunderstanding Caring Leadership**
> When leaders confuse kindness with genuine caring, and fail to establish clear frameworks for decision-making, the entire organizational culture can suffer. Antoine's testimonial illustrates this through a compelling real-world example:
> "For several years, a second secretary had been hired in the company. Limited skills, barely acceptable work quality, and no collaboration with other employees quickly degraded the atmosphere within our company. Despite this, the two bosses did not decide to take appropriate action and kept this person for almost three years (violating the 'no-asshole rule' rule of lever 48). This lack of fairness undermined the managers' credibility and thus the trust relationship.
> This lack of consequences for transgressions creates problems when employees fail to respect the guidelines (which, by the way, have not been clearly defined).
> By confusing *'bienveillance'* (caring) with *'gentillesse'* (kindness), my superiors disregarded the value of fairness. It is interesting to note that after this secretary's departure, the general atmosphere improved significantly. Not only was the person in question no longer harming other employees' work, but trust and respect toward management meant something again."

---

[5] I also like Olivier Truong and Paul-Marie Chavanne's view that "a benevolent attitude towards someone is one that deliberately favors the positive over the negative, the potentials over the shortcomings inherent in that person, with the greatest respect for that person (and first and foremost for their freedom)"; quote from "La bienveillance en entreprise, utopie ou réalité," Eyrolles, 2017.

The absence of clear rules and consistent application created an environment where fairness was compromised. The situation described shows how arbitrary privileges and inconsistent treatment of employees led to deteriorating workplace dynamics. The retention of an underperforming employee who negatively impacted others demonstrates how misguided "kindness" (keeping someone employed despite their harmful behavior) contradicts true caring for the organization and its people.

The leaders' reluctance to address the problematic behavior, likely stemming from misinterpreting caring as mere kindness, ultimately damaged their credibility and eroded trust.

The core challenge in caring lies in how you determine another person's interests. Whenever possible, you should directly engage with individuals who can express their own needs and aspirations. The challenge arises when you believe that you understand someone's interests better than they do themselves. This presents a significant risk: imposing your judgment without a proper foundation.

When you cannot align your understanding with someone's expressed interests, extreme caution and humility become essential. It is often valuable to seek additional perspectives to verify that your understanding of their interests reflects reality rather than your own assumptions or biases.

Clear communication becomes essential in navigating these sensitive situations, although understanding is not always immediate. Sometimes, a person may initially react with anger or resistance, only to realize later that certain tough decisions or actions were in their best interest. This delayed recognition of caring intentions makes it even more important to communicate your reasoning clearly and thoughtfully.

In Practice

True caring sometimes requires actions that may initially appear harsh or unkind but serves a deeper purpose in supporting someone's growth and development. As a teacher, I sometimes deliver incisive criticism aimed at provoking necessary emotional reactions that can catalyze improvement in students' thinking and work quality.

The challenge lies in how this approach can be misinterpreted by students who struggle with criticism. Those lacking self-confidence or possessing inflated egos may view my sharp feedback as a lack of caring, when in fact it represents a deliberate choice to prioritize their learning over their immediate gratification. I gain nothing by causing upset or anger; my demanding approach serves solely to break through the complacency that ultimately hinders their development.

The easier path would be to choose kindness over caring—to be accommodating and avoid criticism. However, this would prioritize my own popularity over students' personal development. By choosing to put students' long-term interests first, even at the risk of their temporary resentment, I demonstrate genuine caring.

This example highlights two crucial aspects of caring leadership: its inherent difficulty and the fact that it may not generate immediate gratitude. True caring requires the courage to make choices that might be initially unpopular but serve others' best interests in the long run.

2.4.2 Do not Forget to Make Your Intention Clear

Since intention is ultimately what matters, clearly communicating that intention becomes vital in caring leadership. Although people may disagree with your approach or views, their perception shifts significantly when they understand your benevolent intent, rather than misinterpreting your actions.

What matters in communication is not what is said, but what is understood. With effective communication and time, those who receive genuine caring often come to recognize and appreciate it, even if they initially resisted or misunderstood the approach.

True caring must be fundamentally selfless. Taking action to benefit others while expecting personal gain is not caring—it is merely seeking a return on investment. Genuine caring means acting purely in others' interests, without seeking personal benefit, compensation, or recognition.

Lever 36 • Act in a Caring Way

True caring requires more than good intentions—it demands concrete actions. Wishing good for others is thus certainly commendable, but it is not enough. Although it is easy to declare noble intentions, credibility comes from making the effort to act on them. Just as environmental concern becomes meaningful only through actions such as waste reduction and resource conservation, caring must be demonstrated through tangible deeds.

Actions speak louder than words because they come with a cost. Words are free, but deeds require effort, time, and often personal sacrifice. Genuine caring typically involves giving up something that serves your own or your organization's interests: spending time helping others can lead to sacrificing time for yourself. Sharing knowledge could imply relinquishing the power of exclusive information. Promoting colleagues could mean that you forego self-promotion opportunities. Teaching others can lead to a sense of surrendering indispensability. Being demanding of others' growth could mean risking your own popularity.

Finding the right balance is essential, as completely sacrificing self-interest is not sustainable or realistic. The key indicator of caring lies in the willingness to partially surrender personal interests for the benefit of others. Even small sacrifices in this direction signal the beginning of genuine caring.

2.4.3   Is It Realistic?

Those who dismiss belief in human caring as naive have fallen into the trap of believing in "survival of the fittest" as the only natural law. As biologists Pablo Servigne and Gauthier Chapelle[6] demonstrate, cooperation, not just competition, is fundamental in nature. Drawing on philosopher Jean-Claude Michéa's work, they expose the historical construction of generalized competition as a founding myth, rather than a natural reality. Their research shows that survivors are not necessarily the strongest, but rather those who help each other most effectively.

Genuine caring is essential for sustainable cooperation. Calculated assistance, offered solely to protect self-interest, is quickly recognized as manipulation and leads only to limited, transactional relationships. As Servigne and Chapelle note, "The sociology of disasters teaches us that social fabric, not material wealth or solid buildings, makes a region resilient. It is the bonds and sense of community that enable weathering of storms."

When their analysis of group resilience is applied to any organization, it becomes clear that caring within an organization contributes significantly to its resilience and, therefore, its longevity. Beyond biological justification and based on practical experience and numerous testimonials, implementing caring leadership is entirely possible, though not necessarily easy or universally achievable.

As not everyone can be caring, organizations would thus benefit from selecting employees who demonstrate capacity for genuine caring, gradually building a more resilient culture. This is a Darwinian approach, which would gradually lead to the exclusion of the less benevolent. At a collective level, both individual organizations and society as a whole can only benefit from increased caring.

Caring is not merely virtuous—it is necessary for maintaining engaged followers over time. As there are enough books extolling the virtues of benevolence, I will refrain from advocating it once again. But to put it bluntly, without it, no employee will want to be engaged. Caring is thus not idealistic thinking but a practical requirement for maximizing performance.

2.4.4   Anchor Caring in the Culture

Leadership sets the tone for organizational culture, but caring must permeate all levels to be sustainable. Although I have previously emphasized the importance of a leader caring about colleagues, this quality must become embedded throughout the organization. A leader practicing caring in isolation, surrounded by noncaring colleagues, risks becoming exhausted, discouraged, and ultimately abandoning the effort. Therefore, it becomes strategically important to recruit employees who naturally demonstrate a caring attitude.

---

[6] Pablo Servigne and Gauthier Chapelle "L'entraide : L'autre loi de la jungle," Les Liens qui libèrent, 2017.

The responsibility falls to managers to cultivate and reinforce a culture of caring within the organization. This involves not only modeling caring behavior but also actively selecting for this quality in hiring/promoting decisions and encouraging its development among existing team members. By consciously building a critical mass of caring individuals, organizations can create a self-reinforcing cycle where caring behavior becomes the norm rather than the exception.

In Practice

Unfortunately, I do not have any miracle recipes for recruiting caring employees. I will only share tips that have generally worked quite well for me: two particularly telling situations often expose a person's capacity for caring:

1. A person's relationship with money reveals a great deal about their character. How someone handles financial interactions, particularly when tipping service workers (while accounting for cultural norms and local customs), can indicate their general disposition toward generosity. This observation stems from the wisdom that those who are tight with money rarely demonstrate generosity in other aspects of life.
2. Treatment of service staff serves as a reliable indicator. How people interact with waiters, secretaries, doormen, concierges, cleaning staff, and other service workers often reveals their true nature. Those who are naturally caring typically demonstrate consistent consideration and spontaneous empathy across all social interactions. Conversely, haughty behavior or dismissiveness toward "subordinate" staff strongly suggests a lack of a caring disposition.

Modern assessment tools offer promising solutions. EazyMirror provides, for instance, a freemium 360° tool that can be customized to measure engagement and other characteristics, including caring. If you prefer to use standard questions, you can use the EazyMirror PFCS survey[7] (Level of Performance, Fairness and Caring) that asks employees to rate the extent to which they feel that:

1. Your direct manager optimizes conditions within their control to enable you and your team to achieve outstanding results
2. Your direct manager (as an individual, independently of their superiors or organizational practices) recruits, promotes, and treats team members and candidates fairly

---

[7] www.EazyMirror.com/PFCS

3. Your direct manager takes action against abuse of power and other transgressions
4. Your direct manager demonstrates genuine care and concern for your well-being

As fair and caring leadership becomes more widespread, implementing the Performance–Fairness–Caring (PFC) model as suggested (see 2.5.3 below) with EazyMirror will enable measurement of each executive's level of caring and fairness. These four scores would be invaluable for assessing each manager's ability to properly balance the PFC model in their managerial practice. The scores will also help each organization to understand how deeply Fair and Caring Leadership is embedded in its culture. Additionally, as they help to gauge the health of organizational culture, these four scores enable executive recruiters to demonstrate to candidates the extent to which the organization walks the talk.

Transparency about caring metrics can serve as a self-selection tool. Informing candidates during recruitment that their level of caring and fairness will be regularly measured through 360-degree assessments if hired can effectively screen out those who know that they do not meet these standards or motivate others to develop these qualities.

You will immediately see the benefits of recruiting caring employees. After all, they will be kind to customers, colleagues, and even you. This can only make your job easier, starting a virtuous circle. Recruiting unsympathetic staff is like shooting yourself in the foot. With them, the result will be the same as putting sand in a ball bearing or a salad.

When employees demonstrate caring toward each other and their managers, conflict decreases, and cross-functional collaboration improves. This naturally enhances collective performance, and customers experience better treatment as well.

As employees spontaneously imitate their leader, you set the tone. Without you walking the talk, there can be no caring culture. You therefore carry a significant responsibility: creating an environment where caring is the rule.

To anchor caring in the culture, you need to elevate it to the level of an imperative, treating it for its own sake rather than just an expected behavior. This is where intention becomes paramount: in whose interest have actions been taken? If it is in the interest of the other person, the imperative of caring has been respected. Any action taken without considering the other person's interests merely mocks the principle of caring.

Maurice's Testimonial: An Engineer's Perspective
"From 2003 to 2011, I worked as an engineer in the R&D department of an industrial company producing automation components. The company was founded by two partners who created a particularly caring working environment conducive to innovation. They were called by their first names: Freddy and Pedro (F&P). The former was in charge of R&D, sales and marketing, whereas the latter managed the other departments. In 2005, the company was sold to a competitor, and they left for good a year later.

I worked at the head office, which employed around a hundred people, a third of whom worked in the various design offices. Most of us were technicians and engineers. I had a direct manager who reported to the department manager, who reported to Pedro.

During this period, I worked on customer projects involving the integration of electronics into existing products to make them "intelligent." I interacted with colleagues from most departments, as well as with some suppliers.

F&P wanted to secure both the economic future of their employees and that of their company (sustainability and security), and to offer employees greater autonomy and self-control. As Freddy explains in his autobiographical work,[8] he had "become convinced that autonomy and self-control were far more profitable and satisfying for employees." He felt that everyone was "an entrepreneur in their own job" who could manage their own time and way of working. So much for the main motivations.

In addition, F&P wanted to remove all frustrating activities that were a source of demotivation and build a friendly working environment ("living well together") without control, authority, or overwhelming supervision (Freddy saw excessive control as a source of unnecessary stress for the employee).

Power sharing was essentially as follows:

- Information sharing: any employee could access most of the company's business information, such as product manufacturing plans, at any time via the open intranet
- Employee empowerment: they encouraged their employees' autonomy and self-control by giving them more responsibilities (empowerment), convinced that they would be more satisfied and more involved (which was indeed the case)
- Team motivation was high: most employees were highly engaged and worked on average more than contractually agreed

---

[8] Freddy Sarfati, "L'Entreprise autrement," L'Harmattan, 2010.

The high level of overall motivation can be explained by the fact that F&P were able to satisfy virtually all the lower levels of Maslow's pyramid, enabling most employees to flourish. Indeed, F&P provided economic security (second level); they succeeded in creating a united (almost tribal) group with which most of us identified and were loyal and proud to belong to (third level). Finally, they regularly showed us their trust and appreciation (fourth level). For example, Pedro was an exemplary leader who visited us often and never lost an opportunity to encourage us, reassure us, congratulate us, or ask us questions on subjects that were important to us, thus increasing our self-esteem, mutual recognition, and involvement. This sense of responsibility and trust was reflected in our almost solitary management of the projects entrusted to us, and in our right to place certain orders without a double signature.

When we received visits from customers or suppliers, the managers regularly came to greet them and exchange a few words, irrespective of their economic weight. This created a cordial and friendly atmosphere and showed their presence (marking their territory).

To facilitate exchanges and enhance our well-being, drinks were provided free of charge, and there was no control over the number and duration of the breaks we took. These breaks were privileged moments for discussion and exchange between colleagues about professional and other situations.

Via the intranet, we had access to an enormous amount of company information. The system was completely open and transparent. The directors were aware that a malicious person could have retrieved the information needed to reproduce the products. However, they felt that a locked system had even more disadvantages. This vote of confidence in us had an important counterpart: it offered the possibility of the documents being supervised by everyone rather than just two or three people, which increased the likelihood that they would be correct. I wonder whether this would still be the case today, especially after the cases of indelicate employees who left with strategic information concerning their company.

This environment of caring, camaraderie, and fraternity created a fertile ground for innovation, resulting in the regular creation of innovative products that won several innovation and design awards.

In conclusion, Freddy and Pedro have succeeded in addressing the four levels of caring (pleasant working conditions, availability and time management, fraternal and constructive behavior and relationships between people, as well as the application of governance rules). In this way, they have created an environment conducive to a high level of employee engagement, which has translated into higher productivity, boosting our competitiveness."

2.5   Bringing the Three Imperatives to Life with the Performance–Fairness–Caring Model

2.5.1   Why Are There Two Imperatives of Fairness and Caring?

Because one without the other can lead to damaging excesses. You can be fair without caring, and vice versa.

If Solomon's decision to cut in two a child that two mothers were fighting over had been implemented, it would undoubtedly have been fair, but clearly not caring.[9] On a more professional note, we might be tempted to reduce the salary of an early retiree who is unable to adapt to new technologies. This would be fair to young people who have mastered them but not caring toward the early retiree. Similarly, we could distribute the same bonus to all employees, regardless of their level of performance. Olivier Truong and Pierre-Marie Chavanne[10] confirm this, pointing out that "being caring does not necessarily mean being conciliatory, or even tolerant. Excessive conciliation and tolerance lead to a form of indifference, which is the opposite of caring."

To avoid this kind of situation, just take the other imperative into account. Deciding to what extent each of these two complementary imperatives should be considered represents a process of arbitration. Difficult as it may sometimes be, this arbitration is nonetheless unavoidable. The point of both imperatives, then, is that one protects against the excesses of the other. As mentioned above, what counts is that people perceive that all parameters have been considered. It is up to each and every one of us to sort things out and justify the basis on which the final decision was taken.

The reason why I have personally concluded that these two imperatives are essential in a professional context is that many expected behaviors result from them. As a result, expected behaviors no longer need to be categorized as imperatives or values:

- Honesty: it is impossible to be dishonest while being fair-minded.
- Integrity: those who demonstrate fairness and caring will not be able to behave without integrity.
- Respect: someone who is caring will automatically be respectful.
- Loyalty: spontaneous loyalty automatically means taking into account the interests of the person to whom you wish to be loyal. On the other hand, there is no caring when loyalty is calculated, notably for fear of possible reprisals.
- Listening: listening means taking things into account. You cannot ignore what people think and say and, at the same time, pretend to be caring, and so on.

---

[9] In this biblical story, King Solomon used this threat to identify the real mother, who would rather give up her child than see it harmed.

[10] Olivier Truong and Paul-Marie Chavanne "La bienveillance en entreprise, utopie ou réalité," Eyrolles, 2017.

Lever 46 • Ensure That the Dignity of Each Person Is Respected

The imperatives of fairness and caring also guarantee the right to dignity of all the organization's employees.[11] With my eminently humanist worldview, I take this right for granted and consider it non-negotiable. Those who are not convinced have bought the wrong book, because it is not aimed at them. A book on the merits of exploitation would suit them much better.

Yet this seemingly self-evident right is flouted on a daily basis in most companies. Every vexation, every humiliation, every abuse of power, every lack of recognition, every discrimination is an example of an attack on the dignity of the employees who suffer them. Donna Hicks points out that, of the ten violations of dignity, the one that affects employees the most, and which is also the most frequent, is a lack of psychological security, in other words, fear. Fear of speaking their mind, fear of abuse of power, fear of reprisals if they report the transgressions that they observe, and so on.

As fear, in one form or another, is unfortunately omnipresent in almost all organizations, it goes without saying that the dignity of employees is also all too often violated. It is unthinkable for employees to be or remain engaged when their dignity is not respected. It appears that attacks on dignity are an obvious factor in disengagement. Guaranteeing their dignity is therefore an inescapable imperative if disengagement is to be avoided.

To minimize damage to dignity, you should put in place rules of governance that prohibit it. This is the vital minimum. However, this minimalist approach does not necessarily imply caring. It is perfectly possible to respect certain rules of governance without being caring, thereby avoiding the sanctions resulting from transgressing them.

On the other hand, fairness and caring ensure that the dignity of your employees is never compromised. Fairness and caring are true guarantees of your team's dignity.

Providing dignity obviously helps to prevent disengagement, but it is not enough to maximize the level of engagement. To get your employees to commit, you also need to arouse their desire to get involved. Your sincere desire for what is best for them will have more impact on their level of engagement than if they think you are doing the bare minimum to protect their dignity. This is why, even if they are the guarantors, fairness and caring go beyond the simple right to dignity.

2.5.2 Become a Fair and Caring Leader

"**The fair and caring leader wins the hearts and minds of employees to achieve an agreed purpose together by balancing the imperatives of fairness and caring with that of performance.**"

---

[11] For detailed explanations of the importance of dignity and the need to ensure it, see Donna Hicks' book "Leading with Dignity: How to Create a Culture That Brings Out the Best in People," Yale University Press, 2018.

Winning hearts requires creating genuine engagement. This occurs through fostering ownership, generating excitement, and inspiring employees to embrace challenges.

Winning minds demands creating shared understanding. Everyone needs clear direction on what should be achieved and how best to do it.[12]

Attempting to achieve objectives without heartfelt support from your teams is futile. Too many managers believe that intellectual convincing is sufficient. They forget that human beings are primarily driven by emotions. Emotions play an essential role in determining engagement levels. You cannot maximize performance while ignoring your employees' emotions—this is an absolute illusion.

Bottom line, the definition breaks down into:

- A primary goal: winning hearts and minds
- An end result: achievement of an agreed purpose
- A type of interaction: collaborative achievement ("together")
- Means: balance of fairness, caring, and performance

2.5.3   The Challenge of Balancing Imperatives

An imperative, by its nature, demands absolute priority. This can become dangerous, acting like a steamroller that crushes everything in its path. We have seen this in practice: collective success used to justify employee burnout, or shareholder value maximization, leaving no resources for employee well-being. The Industrial Revolution exemplifies such excessive deviation, which ultimately led to the emergence of unions as a necessary counterweight.

The counter-example
Here's a situation from a newspaper article:[13]

"With a degree in chemical engineering from EPFL,[14] Camille is one of those rare talents you can trust without hesitation. The feedback from her superiors is excellent, and she is given increasingly important tasks, to the point of excess. Camille finally breaks down while piloting a multimillion-dollar expansion project. She resigned, stating that she could "no longer go on like this." (...)

Camille established herself as an essential team member, eventually assuming her superior's role in strategic meetings and providing training to her colleagues. As her responsibilities grew, she found herself at a loss for where to turn. "I'd been sounding the alarm for a while—I was losing my motivation," she confides. When she discusses these difficulties with her manager, the response is scathing: "Everything is a priority."

---

[12] Adaptation of Les Morgan's definition of leadership.

[13] Article by Florian Delafoi and Adrià Budry Carbó published in *Le Temps*, 24 July 2017.

[14] The Swiss Federal Institute of Technology: the Swiss equivalent of MIT.

The case of Camille illustrates this problem perfectly. Her manager's failure to help her demonstrated a complete lack of caring, prioritizing company success regardless of human cost. The result was not just losing a talented employee—the manager lost credibility as a leader. This likely caused widespread disengagement among other team members who witnessed how Camille was treated and understood their leader's true nature. He most likely not only lost Camille but also any remaining followers.

A balanced trade-off is essential to temper excesses. The imperative of sustainability/performance must be weighed against something else. This "something else" should correspond to the imperatives of fairness and caring. These latter imperatives help to temper the excesses that can arise from prioritizing collective success above all else. The relative weight given to each of these three parameters will be guided by individual sensitivity.

Each imperative must be considered in relation to the others. Emphasizing caring while ignoring performance would be suicidal, just as focusing solely on fairness would be problematic. In a professional environment, every decision must take into account all three parameters—this is precisely why they are called "imperatives."

These three imperatives form what I call the "PFC model", creating a golden triangle of governance where each element moderates the excesses of the others (see Fig. 2.1). True leadership talent lies not just in making these trade-offs but in justifying them convincingly.

Making choices just because one holds a leadership position is easy. The real challenge lies in making the right choices—choices that demonstrate genuine consideration for performance, fairness and caring. The ultimate test is whether these decisions are recognized as fair by those that they affect. This distinction highlights the difference between mere authority and true leadership: while authority can impose decisions, leadership requires making choices that resonate with followers' sense of fairness and demonstrate authentic caring. When decisions are made this way, they earn recognition and acceptance rather than mere compliance.

These imperatives function like a constitution in a legal system. Just as a constitution guides the interpretation of laws that cannot anticipate every situation, these imperatives guide the interpretation of interactions and decisions of the organization and its managers.

Fig. 2.1 The Performance–
Fairness–Caring model: the
golden triangle of governance

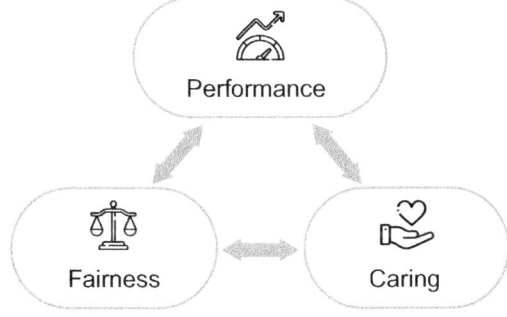

When facing uncertainty or doubt, stakeholders should turn to these three imperatives as their compass to find out if the decision at stake represents a satisfactory balance among the three imperatives. The challenge lies in finding the right, optimal, or just balance among all three imperatives. Like a skilled navigator using multiple reference points, leaders must calibrate their decisions using performance, fairness, and caring as their guiding stars.

When caring and fairness become integral parts of the decision-making equation, they create a protective mechanism for employees. By ensuring that decisions involve a trade-off among all three parameters—performance, fairness, and caring—the risk of excess in any single direction is reduced. This protective mechanism works because it requires leaders to consider the human impact of their decisions alongside organizational performance. The very process of weighing these imperatives against each other helps to prevent the kind of single-minded focus that often leads to employee exploitation or burnout.

Leadership requires employees to want to follow their leader. As a leader, you cannot rely solely on your own worldview; you must test your decisions against your followers' perspectives. If they judge that you are misreading the three imperatives, they will stop following you. When you lose your followers, you lose your leadership.

This creates a challenging balancing act. It demands constant communication to maintain follower engagement while ensuring organizational sustainability. Being and remaining a leader requires mastering this complex dynamic.

> **Testimonial of Claude, Business Controller**
>
> "Early in my career, I was fortunate to have a boss, James, who was an exceptionally caring leader. He was highly intelligent, strategic, and a quick thinker, but what set him apart was his ability to listen and balance needs between the company's interest, himself, and team members, and his ability to put people at ease and give their best.
>
> His approach to problem-solving exemplified true collaborative leadership. Whenever I needed to find a solution to a problem, he would listen to my proposal and process it diligently. He would then ask questions to test my idea, to assess whether it was easy to implement and what the pros and cons were. Sometimes he might have a different approach, but if my idea could work, he would leave me free to choose how to proceed. In cases where James had a better solution than mine, he never imposed it on my proposal, but shared his idea, and we evaluated together how to integrate it with mine to get the best solution.
>
> Even under considerable organizational pressure, James maintained his caring leadership style. He consistently found the time and energy to balance empowerment, coaching, and support for his people.
>
> His long-term perspective shaped how he developed his team. When planning work and allocating tasks, James matched projects to people's interests and aspirations, integrating personal development opportunities into his decision-making process. This seemed very spontaneous, but it was only possible because he knew exactly what people liked and disliked, thanks to frequent informal conversations with his team.

James's leadership embodied the framework of engagement levers. His qualities supported all three imperatives of collective success, fairness, and caring. Although the governance process was not as formalized as the Fair and Caring Leadership Framework suggests, none of the five team members ever felt unclear about objectives or unfairly treated. Whether consciously or unconsciously, his natural behavior aligned with the framework's principles.

His influence continues to shape my approach to leadership. Under his guidance, I became a better decision maker, learning to remain open minded and ready to evaluate and adjust ideas after listening to others' perspectives.

James's authenticity extended beyond his professional role. When he relocated to the USA for a career opportunity, his impact remained. Five years later, when another former team member and I were in California for business, James invited us to his home, where his wife cooked dinner, and we met their children—a final testament to his genuine caring nature."

2.5.4   How to Embody the Three Imperatives

Organizations have mastered performance management but often struggle with fairness and caring. I propose an approach to demonstrate that embodying all three imperatives is achievable.

Like justice, fairness and caring exist primarily in perception rather than absolutes. More or less aware of this major difficulty, people are generally content to verify good intent rather than demanding perfection. They will forgive mistakes or poor choices when made by someone who conscientiously tried their best with available resources and demonstrated genuine intentions to be fair and caring. However, they will not forgive those who make no effort or, worse, display ill intent.

This understanding suggests that embodying these imperatives is not about achieving perfection but rather about demonstrating authentic effort and good faith in balancing all three elements. The key lies in showing genuine commitment to fairness and caring while pursuing performance goals.

In Practice

To ensure you are on the right track, ask yourself these key questions:

1. Have I genuinely considered the other person's interests?
2. What personal or corporate interest did I agree to partially sacrifice for the other?
3. Will my intention be perceived as caring?
4. Do others feel the decision has been made fairly, or at least as fairly as possible?

5. To measure your effectiveness at embodying fairness and caring, you can use the PFCS[15] survey, which complements the one in Sect. 1.3.3:[16] On a scale of 0–4,[17] do you feel that:

   (a) Your leader sincerely strives to be fair?
   (b) Your leader demonstrates authentic caring?
   (c) Your leader takes action against abuse of power?

This stripped-down 360° assessment helps to map how you are perceived.[18] The implementation of this mini-questionnaire requires careful consideration and proper communication. Most importantly, everyone must understand that the approach is governed by two imperatives—fairness and caring—and anyone should be entitled to demand that they are respected.

The EazyMirror PFCS survey can also be used to assess the organization's overall perception of fairness and caring levels. Those who believe that their organization is fair should run this reality check to verify whether their assumption holds true. Management beliefs are one thing, but they need to be confirmed by reality. The PFCS survey is an excellent way of verifying the extent to which employees also believe that they are treated fairly and in a caring manner.

A robust system of safeguards is essential to ensure confidentiality and prevent reprisals and abuse of power in any direction. All violations must be addressed, whether they originate from managers or from subordinates.

If your scores on these assessments are lower than desired, several paths forward exist: seeking personalized development through training or coaching, restructuring your role, enhancing technical expertise while reducing managerial duties, or considering reassignment.

---

[15] Level of Fairness and Caring survey available at https://www.EazyMirror.com/PFCS

[16] A possible variant is the Rotary Club's "4-Way Test," which asks:
   1. Is it the truth?
   2. Is it fair to all concerned?
   3. Will it build goodwill and better friendships?
   4. Will it be beneficial to all concerned?
   https://en.wikipedia.org/wiki/The_Four-Way_Test

[17] Rating Scale
   0 = never
   1 = very little
   2 = little
   3 = quite often
   4 = almost always.
   This scale deliberately omits a middle or "average" option to force respondents to take a clear position. In my humble opinion, any score below 3 should be considered insufficient.

[18] www.EazyMirror.com is an example of a low-cost 360° tool for measuring such perceptions. You can use preset questions or customize your own questions.

Not everyone is naturally suited to team leadership, just as not everyone is meant to be a professional athlete or an auditor. Understanding and accepting this can lead to a more fulfilling career path aligned with your authentic strengths. The key is finding the role that best matches your capabilities and preferences.

2.5.5 The Performance–Fairness–Caring Model Boosts Performance

The Performance-Fairness-Caring model (PFC model) enhances performance by recognizing three essential conditions for employee engagement (see Fig. 2.2 below):

    First, employees must find meaning in their work.

    Second, they must be treated with fairness.

    Third, they must experience genuine caring from leadership.

    These three conditions—Purpose, Fairness, and Caring—work together to drive performance. When all three elements are present, organizations see significantly higher levels of employee engagement and consequently better results.

    The relationship among these three factors and performance is not merely theoretical—it creates a powerful synergy. When employees understand why their work matters, feel that they are treated fairly, and experience authentic caring from leadership, they become genuinely motivated to contribute their best effort.

    Chady's Testimonial below provides compelling evidence that this approach works, even in unexpected environments. Despite the public sector's reputation for traditional management approaches, his experience at the International Trade Centre demonstrates how a single leader can successfully implement these principles. Gerard Lynch's leadership style in a UN organization proves that creating high engagement is possible in any setting when a manager commits to doing what is right.

Fig. 2.2 The performance equation

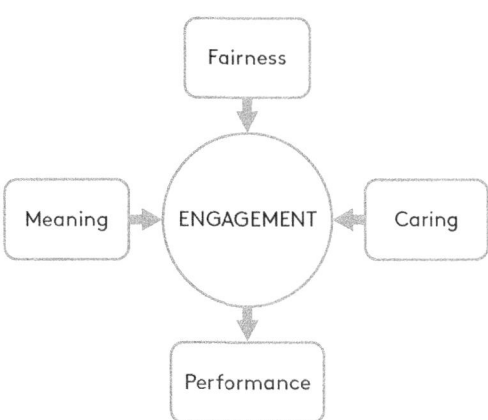

Chady's Testimonial

"From 2013 until 2015 I was blessed to work under the guidance of Mr. Gerard Lynch at the International Trade Centre (ITC), a UN/WTO joint venture here in Geneva. Gerry was the head of the IT department at the time, leading a team of 15 people entrusted with the whole IT infrastructure and systems of ITC, serving around the globe, development projects funded by international donors. Gerry exemplified the good, caring, and fair manager that I strive to become one day. Through his style of coaching combined with a human touch, he managed to rally us behind him and make us deliver goal after goal, achievement after achievement. He set out to define a clear mission for the IT team: promote positive change through technological innovation and lead the way in front of the rest of the organization who are either afraid of speaking up or happy with the status quo. He was passionate about his job and responsibilities, and he channeled this passion to us and reminded us of it day after day. Looking back at it now, I can see that he applied some rules of governance:

- He identified a mission for the team and made sure that we knew it and knew what it meant. He was also someone who was very knowledgeable about the job he was entrusted with; with him an IT strategy was defined for the organization, unheard of before. The strategy set clear measurable targets and outlined the way to reach them. For us employees, it meant that we had a leader with deep knowledge of the subject matter, and subsequently one worry less.
- From the get-go, he had put in place a clear process of promotion based on performance, seniority, and self-development. He made sure everyone who joined was made aware of this and agreed to it. This also meant that he was fair and credible in his assessment; those who merited the promotions based on the criteria that he defined were given the promotions and he pushed for it with management, despite the fact that at ITC one had to go through a competitive selection process to be promoted, even on merit. This made us trust him a little bit more.
- He created a no-fear environment: everyone could speak up and voice their opinion without fear of retribution or judgment. It took a few experiences for this to be "believed" by the staff, such as his accepting criticism or his speaking up to management when he felt that things were unfair.

Among the many traits that I am now able to identify, the one that stands out is his ability to trust us with implementing his vision; As donor funds were allocated to the organization, there was significant pressure to deliver quality projects and products to keep the donors satisfied and keep their money coming back to ITC. And as every project had an IT component, Gerry chose to entrust one member of the team with the project: the expectations were made simple and well communicated to the person responsible for planning, project management, client relationship management (the client was usually an internal ITC division), and implementation. He or she had access to coaching resources from him and other project managers and was trained upon joining the PRINCE2 project management methodology. Apart from this, we were all encouraged to innovate and not to fear experimenting with new technologies as we saw fit, as long as it meant that it could be useful, we could learn from it, and it would help us to deliver what we had to deliver. We all saw in Gerry a father figure: another manager could have cared less about providing us with the tools to do our job better (very common at the UN), but he genuinely cared about our development as much as he did about deliverables; he foresaw training budgets for each of us, even those who were temporary resources; he brought in coaches and training experts to teach us methodologies and skills that we could not afford on our own and which the organization would never bother providing. He contributed to our skills development and employability way beyond what he was asked to. Entrusting us with important projects, delegating management, and empowering us to deliver and improve did not prevent him from recognizing our achievements either: we each had his/her 15 min of fame when releasing products and presenting them to the rest of the organization or the donors; the team member who was in charge of the project had the chance to shine and present their work. As a result, the ITC top management knew each of us by name—uncommon for an IT team—and that made us proud and appreciated."

This real-world example powerfully illustrates that effective leadership transcends organizational constraints. Lynch's success in fostering engagement through clear purpose, fair treatment, and genuine caring validates the practical application of these principles, foreshadowing many of the specific techniques and approaches detailed later in this book.

2.6   Framework for Building Trust, High Engagement, and High Performance

The   Complete Framework for Building Trust, High Engagement, and High Performance (located at the end of the book) **creates key connections between the three core imperatives and practical leadership elements that drive engagement.**
     Each imperative—collective success and organization sustainability, fairness, and caring—is mapped to specific aspects of leadership:

- How leaders should interact with their team members
- Leaders' personality traits that foster engagement
- Conditions that foster engagement

Each element in the book is numbered to correspond with a specific lever in the framework, making it easy to reference and connect concepts. Although the attribution of expectations to specific imperatives represents a considered judgment, these connections remain open to interpretation based on individual perspective.

The Framework for being worthy of trust and obtaining engagement serves as a comprehensive overview of trust-building levers and their roles. For practical application, readers can download a self-assessment version at www.driving-engagement.com/download, allowing leaders to evaluate their implementation of these principles. Note: The categorization of elements under specific imperatives reflects my perceived primary relationships rather than absolute classifications.

In Practice

To begin implementing these principles, start by completing a self-assessment using the downloadable form from www.driving-engagement.com/download. Rate yourself on each dimension using a deliberate four-point scale (0 = not applied, 1 = very inadequate, 2 = inadequate, 3 = very good, 4 = excellent). The scale intentionally omits an "average" option, requiring you to classify your performance as either good (3+) or needing improvement (0–2). A score of 4 indicates minimal room for improvement by any standard.

After completing your self-evaluation and processing its implications, consider gathering feedback from colleagues. Comparing your self-assessment with their perspectives can provide valuable insights. However, their feedback is only meaningful when colleagues feel safe being honest. Use a confidential, anonymous evaluation mechanism such as EazyMirror to ensure candid responses.

Make assessment an ongoing process by periodically repeating these evaluations to track your progress and continued development as a leader.

The Impact of Your Behaviors on Engagement

3

3.1 Your Behaviors Always Impact Your Followers

Your leadership behavior directly influences employee engagement levels through multiple channels. How you interact with team members, make decisions, and demonstrate your commitment to purpose, fairness, and caring shapes their willingness to invest fully in their work.

Understanding this relationship between leadership behavior and engagement is crucial for developing effective leadership practices. The following sections explore specific behaviors that either enhance or diminish engagement, providing practical guidance for leaders seeking to foster higher levels of commitment from their teams.

3.2 So That Imperatives Are Not Just Wishful Thinking

Once defined, imperatives must translate into concrete behaviors to have real impact. Your employees expect alignment between stated principles and actual actions—what can be called "expected behavior." This consistency between words and deeds is fundamental to building trust and credibility as a leader.

Expected behaviors serve as cultural anchors within any community, often understood intuitively by those sharing similar cultural backgrounds. However, in today's increasingly diverse workplace, these expectations can become sources of tension. When team members come from different cultural backgrounds or hold varying interpretations of appropriate behavior, misaligned expectations can easily escalate into disengagement or even conflict.

"Introduction and Warnings" for this book are available in Front matter and "Epilogue" and "Complete Framework for Building Trust, High Engagement, and High Performance" are available in Back matter. Readers can download them free from https://doi.org/10.1007/978-3-032-05172-1.

© The Author(s), under exclusive license to Springer Nature
Switzerland AG 2026
R. H Cohen, *Driving Employee Engagement*, Management for Professionals,
https://doi.org/10.1007/978-3-032-05172-1_3

As organizations actively pursue diversity and multiculturalism, managing these different behavioral expectations becomes increasingly critical. The growing heterogeneity of teams, although beneficial for innovation and perspective, creates fertile ground for potential conflicts unless leaders actively work to establish a clear, shared understanding of expected behaviors.

3.3   Act for Collective Success

Lever 1 • SMART Is Not Enough: Provide Corresponding Resources and Information

Employees need clarity about their objectives and purpose. Changes in direction can be particularly demotivating, especially when they negate previous work and effort. Beyond unpredictable circumstances, seeing their accomplishments rendered meaningless leaves employees with a bitter taste.

Clear, well-thought-out objectives are essential for maintaining employee engagement. Following Boileau's wisdom that "what is well conceived must be clearly stated," managers have a responsibility to carefully consider and explicitly communicate objectives to their teams.

Setting objectives requires more than just making them SMART. You must ensure that goals are not only clear and well-defined but also properly supported by the resources and information needed for success. This comprehensive approach to goal-setting demonstrates respect for employees' efforts and commitment to their success.

Setting clear objectives not only drives collective success but also demonstrates caring leadership. When employees clearly understand what is expected, they waste less time interpreting requirements or redoing misunderstood work. This efficiency shows respect for their time and effort.

Having to redo work owing to poor explanation or planning damages both morale and leadership credibility. Employees interpret such situations either as a lack of caring or managerial incompetence. Either interpretation undermines the manager's standing with their team.

Clear objectives serve multiple purposes: they guide performance, demonstrate respect for employees' time, and establish leadership competence. When managers invest the effort to provide well-defined goals and expectations, they simultaneously support team success and build trust in their leadership capabilities.

Lever 2 • Make Your Expectations Explicit

When I ask managers to describe what they expect from their staff, none of them provides a complete list. I deduce that it is a question that they do not ask themselves or at least do not make a conscious effort to answer. But is it realistic for you to believe that your team members will be able to do exactly what you expect of them if you are not clear about your expectations? The answer is no; it would be unreasonable to expect your direct reports to guess and do what you are unable to formulate.

When I took the trouble to make a list of my expectations, it took me over 18 months to gradually sort out what was important to me. This personal journey revealed the true complexity of defining clear expectations.

When I ask employees, they are unanimous in regretting that their manager has not explicitly defined their expectations. To avoid navigating in uncharted territory, they would like to know what behaviors are expected of them. In other words, employees' legitimate expectations are quite... explicit.

When I reflect on caring leadership, I see that clearly stating your expectations is a fundamental expression of caring. Forcing employees to guess what is expected—under the pretense that it should be "obvious"—leaves them navigating blindly and hoping to find the right path by chance. If it were obvious, I would not have needed 18 months to articulate my expectations, and you would find it easy to list yours. I must ask: is a lack of clarification of expectations truly caring?

The question of fairness is equally critical. How can it be fair to evaluate someone's behavioral performance when you have never clearly communicated what behaviors you expect? I often use this analogy: it is like giving students an exam without telling them the subject matter or assessment criteria. Having tested this scenario myself (and it is indeed an enlightening experiment!), I can confirm that students come away feeling that they have been treated unfairly.

There is also a practical consideration regarding team engagement. If you are implementing the Engaged Team Charter as outlined in Chap. 5, you need to know precisely what you want. When everyone is sharing their expectations, it would be a missed opportunity not to present your own clearly.

My immediate advice: do not waste any time and rush to list your expectations, particularly if, like me, you might need 18 months to have a complete list.

You Can Never Be Too Clear

I love sharing the following story because it perfectly illustrates how even seemingly clear instructions can lead to misunderstandings:

The wife's request "Buy a carton of milk and, if there are eggs, get six" contains an ambiguity that most readers only catch upon second reading. The husband interpreted the instruction literally—since eggs were available, he bought... six cartons of milk!

This anecdote holds a fundamental lesson for leadership communication. What seems crystal clear to you might be interpreted quite differently by others. The wife assumed that her meaning was obvious, just as many managers assume that their expectations are self-evident. Yet the husband's perfectly logical interpretation shows how easily miscommunication can occur.

The story serves as a powerful reminder that clarity in communication requires extra effort. When you share expectations with your team, you must ensure not only that you are being precise but also that your message has been understood as intended. It is not enough to state expectations—you need to verify their interpretation and be willing to rephrase or clarify when needed. The Engaged Team Charter of Chapter 5 is an excellent way to make it happen.

This is why I advocate taking the time to be explicit, even at the risk of seeming redundant. In leadership, as in marriage, you can never be too clear about your expectations.

Lever 3 • Trust Them

I have observed repeatedly that it is futile to expect people to trust you if you do not demonstrate trust in them first. As I explained in Chap. 1, when employees trust their manager, their ability to achieve objectives improves. In other words, for employees to perform well, they must trust you, but for them to trust you, you must trust them first. If you do not trust them, they will not trust you, and their performance will suffer as a result. Bottom line, you have no choice but to trust them.

This creates what I call the trust paradox in leadership:

- You need their trust to get performance
- They need your trust before they can give you theirs
- Therefore, you must initiate trust to enable performance
- Without taking this first step, you cannot unlock their potential

The conclusion is inescapable: as a leader, you must make the first move in establishing trust. It is not optional—it is a fundamental prerequisite for effective leadership. Waiting for team members to prove themselves trustworthy before extending trust creates a deadlock that undermines performance from the start.

Rather than seeing trust as something to be earned over time, it must be offered as an initial investment in the relationship. The returns on this investment—in terms of engagement, performance, and mutual respect—make it not just worthwhile but essential. This insight fundamentally reshapes not only how we must think about trust in organizations but also how we hire employees.

In my experience, retaining team members you do not trust is an exercise in self-punishment. You find yourself compelled to provide exhaustively detailed instructions, constantly anticipating potential problems, and maintaining vigilant control over every aspect. This approach not only complicates processes but also consumes an excessive amount of time and energy. The cost of distrust is substantial. Beyond simple repetitive tasks (which will soon be automated anyway), it is far more efficient to leverage people's intelligence and capability.

One of the unavoidable questions that should drive the recruitment process is "Do I feel comfortable enough with this candidate to trust them first?" This question fundamentally shifts the traditional recruitment paradigm. Instead of focusing solely on skills and experience, I suggest that you must evaluate your own capacity to extend trust to the candidate from day one.

The next question naturally follows: "Will they be compatible enough with the rest of the team so that the other team members will also trust them first?" This consideration acknowledges that trust must operate not just vertically between manager and employee, but horizontally across the entire team. Team dynamics and cultural fit become primary considerations in the selection process.

These questions challenge traditional recruitment practices in several ways:

- They prioritize interpersonal dynamics over technical qualifications
- They recognize trust as a prerequisite rather than as an outcome

- They consider the collective impact on team trust, not just individual capability
- They require the interviewer to examine their predisposition to trust

This approach to recruitment represents a significant shift in mindset. Rather than asking, "Can I trust this person after they prove themselves?" you must ask, "Am I ready to trust this person from day one?" If the answer is no, then regardless of their qualifications, they may not be the right fit for a team that depends on mutual trust to function effectively.

However, trust does not equate to blind faith. As human error is inevitable, it remains prudent to conduct periodic checks to ensure that operations are proceeding smoothly and implement corrections when necessary. This is where the power of teamwork becomes evident—team members supporting each other can compensate for individual mistakes, weaknesses, or shortcomings. Through this collaborative approach, the team's collective performance is optimized.

The beauty of mutual trust lies in its ability to create a virtuous cycle. When you trust your team members, they typically rise to meet that trust with increased responsibility and engagement, which in turn validates and strengthens the trust you placed in them initially.

As I have observed, no one—including managers—is infallible. This reality demands a clear right to make mistakes to be established, ensuring fair treatment for those who act in good faith and for the collective benefit. But I believe that you can go further than merely permitting mistakes—you can even celebrate them. I am particularly inspired by organizations such as Stora Enso that actively reward the most instructive failures—those that generate valuable learning opportunities. This approach represents a powerful vote of confidence and brilliantly encourages constructive initiative, directly contributing to collective success.

However, I must emphasize that trust cannot be unlimited. A framework is essential to define boundaries and expectations. This is precisely where the Engaged Team Charter becomes important—it establishes specific measures at the team level to foster trusting collaboration. The charter should explicitly address the right to make mistakes and clearly define its scope.

The framework serves multiple purposes:

- It provides psychological safety for team members to take calculated risks
- It defines the boundaries between acceptable mistakes and unacceptable errors
- It establishes how learning from mistakes will be captured and shared
- It creates clarity around accountability and responsibility

This structured approach to trust and mistake-making creates a safe environment where innovation can flourish while maintaining necessary safeguards. When team members understand both their freedoms and their responsibilities, they can act with confidence and purpose.

Trust means not only recognizing the intellectual abilities of others but also giving them the opportunity to exploit them. A lack of trust in a collaborator is obviously not flattering and cannot be seen as caring. This fundamental truth challenges us to examine how you assign and empower your team members.

As not everyone has the capacity to do everything, you obviously need to assign responsibilities to each collaborator according to their skills and abilities. You can then trust them within the defined scope. If you do not trust them, it is because you have doubts about whether they are in the right place, and so it is your own decision to have entrusted them with the job that is the problem.

This insight leads to several important conclusions:

- Misalignment between role and capability is more a leadership failure than an employee failure
- Trust must be accompanied by appropriate role assignment and a clear framework defining the rules of the game
- When trust is lacking, leaders should first examine their own decisions
- The right person in the wrong role undermines both trust and performance

The responsibility ultimately lies with leadership. If you find yourself unable to trust an employee, the critical question is not "What is wrong with them?" but rather "Did I make the right decision in assigning them to this role?" This shift in perspective places the burden of creating conditions for trust squarely on leadership's shoulders.

Lever 4 • Share Information and Knowledge

Decompartmentalization and cross-lateral interactions are important optimization factors for organizational success. When I talk about decompartmentalization, I am referring to the sharing of information and knowledge. When the left hand does not know what the right hand is doing, optimal results become impossible. I have witnessed extreme cases—two people working for months in the same room on identical projects, completely unaware of the duplication. Beyond the frustration of this discovery, it represented an obvious waste of resources. These employees understandably developed a poor opinion of their manager, who had allowed this waste to occur. The lack of communication directly translated into inefficiency.

Although information and knowledge sharing clearly promote collective success, I acknowledge that it sometimes needs moderation when confidentiality plays a strategic role. However, this is the exception rather than the rule. The "need to know" approach to sharing information and knowledge makes a problematic assumption—that someone is coordinating everything so perfectly that players in the system do not need to think for themselves. Although possible in theory, this proves difficult and inefficient in practice.

Beyond the often dubious excuse of confidentiality, I frequently encounter the argument that "information is power." The selfish interest behind information hoarding is so obvious that it hardly needs an explanation. Although this withholding undermines collective success, it remains an endemic reality in many organizations.

This resistance to sharing creates a leadership challenge: how to foster a culture where information flows freely while respecting necessary confidentiality boundaries. The solution lies in creating systems, rules, and incentives that reward sharing rather than hoarding information.

The best proof of this dysfunction is that organizational strategy is rarely known, let alone understood, at the lower levels of the pyramid. In my interactions with middle managers, I observe that the further down the hierarchy you go, the less people know about strategy. This translates directly into a lack of alignment and efficiency.

Beyond its negative impact on performance, withholding information and knowledge demonstrates a clear lack of caring. Sharing information helps others to better understand and navigate their environment. To help them is to show them caring. Withholding useful information is a form of malice. The most malicious form appears when only the minimum information is shared, based on what each employee "needs to know." The assumption here is that they cannot be trusted with more information. It obviously reflects a level of trust close to zero...

As mentioned in the section on fairness, anything that can be shared requires the definition of sharing criteria. Defining these criteria is at the heart of the fairness issue. As information and knowledge are eminently shareable, they must be shared equitably.[1] The team charter recommended in Chap. 5 also provides an excellent framework for spelling out these rules of the game when it comes to managing information and knowledge.

This creates three imperatives for leaders:

- Share strategic information broadly throughout the organization
- Establish clear, equitable criteria for information sharing
- Use the team charter to codify information-sharing practices

The goal is not just better performance, but creating an environment of trust where information flows freely and fairly.

Not Sharing Information Is Expensive
Tom and Jane hired a pilot to fly them to Canada to hunt elk. By the end of the day, they had brought back six elk, even though the legal limit was one each. As they began loading the plane for the return trip, the pilot informed them that the plane could only carry four elk. The two hunters objected strongly: "Last year we shot six too, and the pilot let us put them all on board; he had the same plane as you."

Reluctantly, the pilot gave in, and the six elk were loaded on board. However, even at full power, the little plane could not cope with the load and crashed a few moments after take-off.

Emerging from the wreck, Jane asks Tom, "Do you know where we are?"

"Yeah, I think we are pretty close to where we crashed last year."

Besides showing what happens when only part of the information is shared, this story delivers another sobering truth: when you fail to share information about your mistakes and failures, you doom others to repeat them. The cost of such information hoarding is not just financial—it can be dangerous and potentially catastrophic.

---

[1] See the link to informational justice: https://en.wikipedia.org/wiki/Organizational_justice

Lever 5 • Attract and Develop Talents

Leadership is not a solitary endeavor—your success and collective success depend directly on the talents that comprise your teams. To maximize performance, you need to have the most talented team possible. Surrounding yourself with people who are better qualified or even brighter than you is the best guarantee of success (provided that they are engaged!).

To build a high-performing team, there are two fundamental requirements: attract talent and keep it. If you succeed in attracting talented individuals but fail to retain them, it signals a failure to satisfy their expectations.

Sometimes this inability to retain talent is circumstantial, particularly when the organization does not offer sufficient prospects for the future. In these cases, it is not you who fails to retain but the organization. However, there are many cases where the manager is nevertheless the cause of the departure, even if the organization has some responsibility. It is up to you to assess where the responsibility lies.

Even without prospects of progression, you can still attract talent for a limited period. This is far better than surrounding yourself with mediocre people who will undermine your performance. As proof of true caring and taking into account the interests of my team members, I have, on several occasions, encouraged talented individuals to leave my team when I saw that an opportunity presented to them was in their best interest. Even though it would have served my interests to convince them to stay, I chose not to, because privileging my interests over theirs would have demonstrated a lack of caring.

The best way to attract and retain talent is to encourage them to identify and exploit opportunities within your organization that align with both their aspirations and organizational needs. It is like inviting them to create their own jobs. This approach not only engages talented individuals but also drives innovation and ensures your organization's future growth. Levers 39 to 42 in Chap. 5 provide specific tools to implement this strategy.

When talent leaves, you must replace it with new talent. This requires extra effort on your part, but the end result will be much better than if you give up on attracting talent altogether.

Your professional expertise alone is not enough to attract and retain talent. It may attract the most determined individuals, who will come to benefit from your knowledge, but if they are not treated the way they expect to be treated, they will depart as soon as they have absorbed enough of your knowledge.

To assess managers' ability to attract and retain talent, ask employees a simple question: "On a scale of 0 to 4, how good do you think your manager is at attracting and retaining talent?"

Consider making these scores transparent in your recruitment efforts. Strong leaders should embrace this level of openness. Many professions already operate with public ratings—take RateMyProfessors.com, for example, which claims ratings for 1.7 million teachers and attracts more than 4 million visitors. As employees are effectively your customers, publishing manager ratings is not far-fetched. Even if you are not ready to make these scores public, operate as if they were—this mindset will drive you to excel in attracting talent.

Lever 6 • Ask Yourself the Leader's Eight Questions

These questions are fundamental to effective leadership and are thoroughly explored in Chap. 5, where their significance and practical application will be explained in detail. Each question is designed to help leaders to evaluate and improve their leadership approach, but their full context and justification require the foundation that is built through the preceding chapters.

3.4   What You Need to Do for Fairness

Lever 7 • Walk the Talk

Sun Tzu's assertion that "a leader leads by example, not by force" remains profoundly relevant today, despite being articulated over 2000 years ago. This ancient wisdom serves as a reminder that effective leadership is not about coercion but inspiration. This enduring principle highlights a fundamental truth about human nature and leadership that transcends time and culture. The persistence of this principle across centuries raises a critical question: if this wisdom has been known for so long, why do leaders still struggle to embody it?

Exemplary leadership is universally recognized as a must, yet its absence remains a persistent problem in organizations. The "do as I say, not as I do" approach is not just ineffective—it is an insult to employees' intelligence. Despite this obvious truth, many managers would not dare to admit it, but they continue to lack exemplarity, acting as if others are too stupid to notice.

This attitude shows a profound disrespect for their colleagues' intelligence. The reality is that this behavior persists because those around them are powerless—aside from their superiors, employees have no recourse when faced with a manager who abuses their power to grant themselves privileges.

Lack of exemplarity fundamentally communicates that someone considers themselves above the rules that govern others. Unless you accept the problematic notion of inherently superior and inferior beings, this behavior is a clear manifestation of inequity. The only legitimate exceptions to rules are those explicitly built into the rules themselves—in which case, following these exceptions is adhering to the rule, not breaking it.

Outside of explicitly authoritarian systems such as monarchies or dictatorships, equality before rules should be universal. When leaders grant themselves the privilege of disregarding rules, they effectively declare themselves privileged without consensus. This self-assigned exceptional status creates problems when others do not share or accept this presumption of privilege.

When you do not follow rules, you invalidate those very rules for everyone else. This creates a logical contradiction that undermines your authority: if you consistently arrive late while demanding punctuality from others, you are demonstrating through your actions that the rule is not important. This behavior:

- Invalidates the rule through the leader's example
- Removes the leader's legitimacy to enforce the rule
- Creates a sense of inequity that damages organizational culture
- Undermines the entire system of organizational rules and expectations

The result is a breakdown in organizational order and a justified resistance to leadership authority.

The same principle applies in educational settings, where students readily point out that teachers demanding respect must first demonstrate respectful behavior themselves. This reflects a broader truth about the reciprocal nature of respect and authority. It is particularly noteworthy that Millennials show significantly less tolerance for leadership privileges than previous generations. If you are hoping that your lack of exemplary behavior will be accepted by your Millennial employees, you are making a serious miscalculation. This generation's heightened sensitivity to fairness and consistency means they are more likely to:

- Question authority that does not demonstrate consistent standards
- Challenge leadership behaviors that contradict stated values
- Disengage when they perceive double standards
- Seek employment elsewhere when faced with non-exemplary leadership

The fact that leaders who fail to demonstrate exemplarity can get away with such behavior reveals a fundamental flaw in organizational power structures. This troubling reality exposes how traditional organizational hierarchies often lack the necessary mechanisms to enforce accountability at leadership levels. When leaders can consistently act without exemplarity and face no consequences, it indicates a systemic failure rather than just individual misconduct.

This underlines that relying solely on individual leaders' self-regulation is insufficient to maintain equity and prevent the abuse of power.

Just acknowledging the importance of exemplary leadership is also not enough—organizations need robust governance that ensures that leaders cannot exempt themselves from the standards that they impose on others. When leaders assume that their inconsistencies go unnoticed or believe that they can act with impunity, they not only undermine their own credibility but also damage the trust in the organization. The persistence of such behavior despite its obvious visibility to employees creates a toxic environment where cynicism can flourish.

The solution requires both structural changes and individual accountability.[2] Organizations need systems that allow employees to safely challenge leadership behaviors that contradicts stated values,[3] whereas leaders must commit to genuine self-reflection and consistent modeling of the standards that they expect from others.

The root cause of non-exemplary leadership lies in a fundamental structural problem: when a single individual holds both the power to make decisions and

---

[2] See Lever 47.

[3] Concrete and practical ways to implement such systems will be presented in my upcoming book "*La Sécurité Psychologique en Entreprise*".

judge their fairness, the potential for misuse becomes significant. In other words, when leaders hold both executive and judicial power without adequate checks and balances, the temptation to rule by force rather than by example becomes harder to resist.

The antidote to this concentration of power is an effective internal justice system.[4] Such a system provides the necessary counterbalance to leadership authority by:

- Separating executive and judicial functions within the organization
- Creating formal channels for addressing grievances
- Establishing independent oversight of leadership behaviors
- Ensuring accountability at all levels of the organization

Bottom line, your actions as a leader speak louder than your words or your formal authority. When you lead by example, you demonstrate respect for both the rules and the people you lead, creating a foundation for genuine organizational equity.

The message is clear: modern leadership requires genuine commitment to walking the talk, as younger generations will not accept the traditional "do as I say, not as I do" approach.

The boss sets the example

Believing that the organization needed to be culturally energized, the board of General Machines Corp hired a new president who was determined to eliminate underperforming employees.

While visiting the factory, the president notices a man leaning against a wall, arms crossed. The room is filled with employees. He thinks to himself, "I will show them I mean business!" He approaches the man, "How much do you earn per week?"

Somewhat surprised, the young man looks at him and replies, "I earn $400 per week, why?"

The president responds, "OK, do not move from there!"

He returns to his office, comes back 2 min later and hands him $1600 in cash, adding, "Here is four weeks' salary, now get out and do not come back!"

Proud of having sent a symbolic message, the president looks around and asks, "Can anyone tell me what this lazy incompetent was doing here?"

From the other end of the room, a small voice answers, "That is the guy who was waiting to be paid for the pizza we ordered!"

This anecdote perfectly illustrates how rushing to judgment and attempting to demonstrate authority through dramatic gestures can backfire spectacularly, undermining leadership credibility and creating exactly the opposite effect from what was intended.

---

[4] See my article entitled "La justice, talon d'Achille des organisations," Expansion Management Review, September 2010.

Lever 8 • Balance the Four Fundamental Interests (Personal, Employer, Employees, Civil Society)

A manager must skillfully balance four essential interests to achieve effective leadership:

First, the organization's interests must be protected. A manager who fails to serve their employer's objectives risks termination. This includes:

- Delivering expected results through consistent performance and achievement of established targets
- Supporting shareholder and owner interests by protecting and growing organizational value
- Maintaining organizational sustainability through sound decision-making and resource management
- Demonstrating value for compensation received, which demonstrates fairness toward the employer and its shareholders

Second, personal interests remain legitimate. As you are not expected to be Mother Teresa, you need not sacrifice your well-being entirely—it is, for instance, reasonable and fair to also pursue:

- Career advancement
- Fair compensation
- Professional satisfaction
- Personal development

Third, team members' interests require careful consideration. This forms a core component of Fair and Caring leadership through:

- Supporting team development through consistent opportunities for learning and advancement that help colleagues to reach their full potential
- Ensuring fair treatment by maintaining equitable practices in assignments, recognition, and rewards across all team members
- Promoting workplace well-being by creating an environment where colleagues feel psychologically safe and supported
- Fostering collaborative growth by encouraging teamwork and mutual support that benefits both individual and collective development

Fourth, social responsibility demands attention. This increasingly important dimension includes:

- Environmental-impact consideration
- Community-effects evaluation
- Employment-impact assessment
- Ethical decision making

The true art of leadership lies in achieving a just harmonization of these four fundamental interests without completely sacrificing any single one. This delicate balancing act requires careful consideration and continuous adjustment to maintain organizational health while demonstrating both fairness and caring.

These four interests represent key stakeholders: the employer, the manager, the employees, and civil society (including environmental concerns). Overemphasizing any single interest risks provoking resistance from neglected stakeholders. The easiest yet most dangerous path is sacrificing employee interests, as they often appear to be the most expendable stakeholders.

Do not fall into the trap of undervaluing employees' interests, for several compelling but misguided reasons. The negative impacts are not immediately visible, and employees seem easier to replace than other stakeholders. Leaders often mistakenly believe that compensation can offset unfairness, whereas short-term financial results may temporarily mask deeper problems.

However, this approach inevitably fails for fundamental reasons. Trust, once broken, is extremely difficult to rebuild, and financial incentives only boost motivation for up to 3 months. Employees who feel sacrificed once will never fully trust you again, and the resulting disengagement creates lasting damage that permeates throughout your organization.

The only viable solution is to achieve genuine balance among all stakeholders. Although this is challenging, it represents the essence of true leadership. Success requires exceptional talent for stakeholder management, combined with wisdom in balancing competing interests. You must develop skill in managing various stakeholder perceptions while maintaining an unwavering commitment to consistent fair treatment.

No one claims that leadership is easy, but sacrificing employee interests for expedience ultimately undermines the foundation of organizational success. The true measure of leadership lies in your ability to navigate these competing interests while maintaining trust and engagement across all stakeholder groups.

In Practice

This just balancing act requires:

- Recognizing when interests compete or align
- Making transparent trade-offs when necessary
- Ensuring that no single interest consistently dominates
- Creating sustainable solutions that serve multiple interests simultaneously

The resulting just arbitration demonstrates leadership excellence through:

- Fair consideration of all stakeholders
- Caring attention to the impact on all parties
- Sustainable approaches that maintain long-term viability
- Ethical decision making that builds trust

When you achieve this just harmonization, you create an environment where organizational success, personal growth, colleague well-being, and social responsibility reinforce rather than undermine each other. This balance becomes self-sustaining as each stakeholder group sees its interests being fairly considered and protected.The challenge lies in managing interests that do not naturally align. Consider environmental protection: installing pollution control equipment is costly and seemingly conflicts with organizational profitability and shareholder interests. Yet, continuing to pollute threatens long-term sustainability and shareholder value. This illustrates how environmental, social, and governance decisions reflect underlying intentions—you might invest in environmental protection out of genuine ecological concern, to safeguard long-term shareholder interests, or merely for greenwashing.

The same principle applies to collaborator treatment. You can care for your teams with a purely utilitarian mindset: happier employees generate higher productivity and profits. Alternatively, as a fair and caring leader, you might prioritize their well-being because you genuinely care about them as people, not just resources.

Your intention—the "why" behind your actions—makes all the difference. Your teams will judge you based on their perception of whose interests you serve. This makes it crucial to clearly communicate the reasoning behind your decisions. The fundamental question remains: whose interests drove this choice, and what imperative guided it?

Viewing employees merely as means to achieve organizational goals, rather than as people, reveals a fundamental lack of caring. This mindset reduces human beings to mere resources serving your success. When you see people as means to an end, your "talent" becomes nothing more than efficiently exploiting them, replacing those who burn out like worn-out machinery.

This "expendable workforce to be exploited" mentality might make you an efficient resource manager, but it disqualifies you as a leader. Although you might excel at managing resources, true leadership requires more. Remember: leadership exists only when there are engaged followers, and Fair and Caring Leadership demands genuine consideration of team interests.

As a leader seeking engaged followers, you have no alternative. You must consistently demonstrate that team interests factor into every decision. Once your people doubt your commitment to their welfare, your leadership crumbles.

Lever 9 • Ensure the Safety and Well-Being of Your Employees

Whether you like it or not, the employer–employee relationship inherently involves subordination. In Swiss law, as well as in many other legal systems, this subordination or dependency relationship serves as a key differentiator between employed and self-employed status. This structure grants managers greater decision-making authority and strategic visibility than their employees.

Employees face inherent vulnerability owing to information and power asymmetry. With limited access to information, comprehensive knowledge, and decision-making authority, employees must trust their managers to make sound decisions, particularly regarding job security.

Management failures in anticipating challenges directly impact trust. Except in very unforeseeable circumstances or situations of force majeure, downsizing measures can indicate management's failure to anticipate and prevent problems. This raises a critical question: how can employees maintain trust in leaders who failed to protect their positions?

Protecting employee interests requires active leadership engagement. Taking responsibility means fighting for jobs and nurturing employees' self-worth. Maintaining trust demands visible effort in protecting employment security.

A Fair and Caring leader prioritizes employees' well-being through actions, not just words. Success depends on employees' perception of fairness and caring, manifested through good working conditions. When organizations face difficulties, employees willingly make sacrifices if they perceive fair treatment throughout the process.

In Practice

If you genuinely care about your employees' interests, you must recognize your role as a guardian of job security. The trust that employees place in their leaders directly correlates with their perception of your efforts to protect employment and the concrete results achieved.

Failed leadership has lasting consequences for trust. When you maintain your position and compensation while your teams face downsizing owing to poor strategic decisions, you severely damage trust. Surviving team members who witness colleagues losing jobs because of management's lack of foresight will not perceive this as fair treatment.

Employee assessment of leadership never stops. Your teams continuously evaluate your level of caring and fairness through your visible efforts to protect their well-being and employment security. This perception fundamentally shapes their trust in you, directly affecting their engagement levels and ultimate performance.

Lever 10 • Renounce Paradoxical Injunctions

Beyond poor leadership exemplarity, paradoxical injunctions rank among the most damaging management practices. These contradictory demands include "doing more with less," increasing customer availability while expanding administrative duties, improving service quality with reduced staff, and finding solutions without adequate resources.

Encouraging employees to exceed their potential is admirable, but reason must prevail. Demanding what lies beyond a collaborator's capabilities creates feelings of incompetence and injustice, demonstrating neither caring nor fairness. It also undermines their confidence. Such demands place employees in situations of programmed failure and unnecessarily elevate their stress levels beyond what is reasonable.

Paradoxical injunctions erode trust in management capabilities. Leaders who make unrealistic demands reveal either a fundamental misunderstanding of operations or an inability to grasp field-level realities. When employees dare to highlight these impossible expectations, dismissive responses such as "figure it out yourself" only confirm management's unwillingness to listen and tendency to avoid reality. Such behavior raises serious doubts about leadership's discernment abilities and decision-making competence.

Such leadership behavior destroys credibility and trust. Could you reasonably expect to maintain team confidence while issuing impossible demands? Of course not! These paradoxical injunctions act as an invisible poison, steadily eroding engagement levels throughout the organization.

Despite their destructive nature, paradoxical injunctions remain widespread. Many managers appear blind to how these impossible demands damage both employee engagement and their own credibility. Their denial is often interpreted as either deliberate avoidance of responsibility or susceptibility to unrealistic aspirations.

Some may view driving impossible excellence as a path to heroic leadership status. However, this pursuit of glory through team suffering ultimately fails. Employees readily see through such theatrical management, rejecting both the performance and its director.

In Practice

Given management's apparent susceptibility to issuing paradoxical injunctions and their damaging effect on engagement, preventive measures are essential. An Engaged Team Charter should include specific governance rules that prohibit and expose such contradictory demands. Teams might, for instance, designate specific individuals as being responsible for identifying paradoxical injunctions and bringing them to the attention of others.

Feedback interviews provide valuable opportunities to address these issues. Bringing them up openly and discussing with management the difficulty created by paradoxical injunctions should be the simplest and easiest way to address them. For this to happen, there should be enough psychological safety so that no one is afraid to speak up. When participants approach these discussions with genuine good faith, they can work together to develop practical solutions that avoid impossible demands. This collaborative approach helps to maintain trust while ensuring that expectations remain reasonable and achievable.

Consequences of Paradoxical Injunctions
A couple, under stress after a quarrel, had agreed to communicate only in writing.

The day before, the husband wrote: "Wake me up at 7 a.m."

At 10 a.m. the next morning, he woke up furious and saw a note at the bedside: "Get up! It's 7 a.m."

This anecdote perfectly illustrates the absurdity of paradoxical injunctions. The wife technically followed the letter of the request while completely undermining its spirit. She created a situation where compliance with the instruction made its actual purpose impossible to achieve.

Lever 11 • Recognize Everyone's Contribution...

Among the major sources of employee frustration, alongside leadership failures and paradoxical injunctions, lies the widespread lack of recognition. This deficiency ranks as a primary cause of workplace dissatisfaction.

The reasons behind this recognition deficit matter less than addressing its existence. What matters is acknowledging this perception and taking decisive action to reduce it. Employees demonstrate a profound hunger for recognition, which aligns with fundamental human psychology. This desire for acknowledgment connects directly to self-esteem needs, positioned prominently in Maslow's hierarchy of needs.

In Practice

As employees with high (but not inflated) self-esteem perform better and experience greater satisfaction, developing their sense of worth should be your priority. Research confirms that content employees enhance organizational profitability and creativity. Yet beyond these utilitarian benefits, a Fair and Caring leader who genuinely values employee interests must take necessary steps to ensure that team members feel appreciated and valued.

Acknowledging achievements is fundamentally a matter of fairness. It requires explicit appreciation of each person's contribution. Those who underperform must face consequences owing to their accountability. Symmetrically, high performers deserve recognition for their superior contributions—this represents basic fairness.

Your legitimacy to address shortcomings depends on your willingness to acknowledge successes. When you demonstrate the ability to recognize both achievements and areas for improvement, your team sees your capacity for balanced judgment. This measured approach, combining discernment with wisdom, encourages trust in your leadership decisions.

In Practice

As recognition builds staff self-esteem, seize every opportunity to express your appreciation for what your team members have done.

Recognition must flow from genuine sincerity, as inauthentic appreciation destroys trust. Recognition follows the same principles as rewards: It must be proportional, justified, justifiable, and timely.

Public recognition carries greater impact than private acknowledgment. Expressing appreciation before others creates a multiplier effect. However, verify individual preferences first, as not everyone welcomes public recognition.

The more personal the expression of gratitude, the greater its impact. A handwritten note carries significantly more weight than an email or text message.

Although most organizations tend to privilege the recognition of results and outcomes, they should also pay attention to all categories of recognition, particularly those that extend beyond mere results. Focusing primarily on results prevents you from acknowledging other important aspects of recognition:

- Recognition of expertise: acknowledge professional know-how and business acumen, even when results fall short. This validates craftsmanship, talent, and skill
- Recognition of effort: honor the investment, dedication, and sacrifices made, regardless of outcome
- Existential recognition: simple acts such as greetings, information sharing, meeting invitations, and scheduled appointments acknowledge a person's fundamental value and organizational role

Lever 11 • ...and Reward Those Who Deserve It

The question of reward carries significant emotional weight, intertwining with recognition and monetary compensation. Money represents access to desired things. Although the topic is broad, I will focus on its connection to Fair and Caring leadership.

People always evaluate rewards through the lens of fairness. Success naturally leads to positive recognition. Regarding compensation, while everyone desires higher earnings, experience suggests that people primarily seek fair rewards. The critical question becomes: What criteria do they use to determine fairness in their eyes?

Fairness exists only through perception rather than through absolute measures. Employees evaluate their compensation through two primary comparisons: their market value and their colleagues' compensation for similar roles and performance. Given the subjective nature of these assessments, no universal solution exists.

I believe that a third fundamental factor influences compensation perception: the overall impression of leadership fairness and caring. When employees view their manager as fundamentally fair and caring, they extend trust to compensation decisions. Conversely, those who doubt their manager's fairness feel compelled to verify their compensation against market rates and peer salaries.

Employee trust in management remains central to all workplace interactions. Your trustworthiness depends entirely on your consistent behaviors. Employees continuously evaluate your actions to assess your level of fairness and caring. This constant observation means that you must maintain unwavering commitment to these principles.

Beyond basic compensation, rewards must recognize exceptional effort and results. Excellence deserves acknowledgment—a fundamental matter of fairness. Yet determining reward parameters presents challenges in objectivity. Success requires transparency about expectations, achievement gaps, and assessment methods.

The perception of fairness develops long before specific reward decisions arise. Although stakeholder attitudes and mutual perceptions of fairness play crucial roles in reward discussions, these perceptions form through previous demonstrations of caring and fairness. By the time that reward decisions occur, trust levels have already been established through past leadership behavior.

As your actions and decisions are constantly scrutinized by your team members, there is no respite for those in leadership. In other words, the painful truth is that there are no "off days" when it comes to demonstrating fair and caring leadership. You must maintain unwavering dedication to their principles, as any deviation can impact trust and engagement.

In Practice

I believe that rewards must follow three essential criteria to be effective. They should be:

- Justified by explicit criteria (preferably based on independent external standards)
- Proportional to maintain fairness
- Timely in their delivery. A delayed reward has already created bitterness between the moment it was expected and the moment it was received. This undermines the positive intent behind the reward.

Poor reward decisions can severely damage managerial credibility. Disproportionate or unjustified rewards reveal poor judgment and disconnect from reality, making it difficult for team members to trust the leader's decision-making abilities. True fairness requires both rewarding deserving performance and withholding rewards when unwarranted.

Generic rewards often backfire. Standard gifts, such as 10-year service pens, typically fail to resonate with employees. These impersonal gestures, though well-intentioned, can generate resentment rather than appreciation, particularly when delivered without thoughtful consideration.

Financial incentives have limited motivational impact. As the effect of monetary rewards and salary increases on motivation typically last no more than 3 months, these should be viewed as fair compensation adjustments rather than motivational tools.

Personalized rewards create lasting impact. Understanding what really matters to each individual should provide you with clues for meaningful recognition that will be appreciated. Opera tickets for a music enthusiast or flexible scheduling for parents with young children can have far greater value than traditional monetary rewards. This personalized approach demonstrates both caring and attention to individual preferences.

3.5   Embodying Caring

Lever 12 • Empower People

Although empowerment has become a prevalent concept in management discourse, the distinction between delegation and empowerment remains frequently misunderstood.

Delegation transfers responsibility for execution while retaining decision-making authority at the delegating level. The person receiving the delegation must act within prescribed boundaries and often needs to seek approval for significant decisions or resource requirements. They become responsible for achieving outcomes without necessarily having control over the means of achieving them.

True empowerment combines responsibility with genuine decision-making authority. An empowered individual or team receives both the accountability for results and the autonomy to determine how to achieve them, including control over necessary resources. This encompasses the authority to make strategic choices, allocate resources, and select methods without constant reference to higher levels of management.

The sales manager scenario illustrates this distinction. When assigned a 10% sales increase target without the authority to adjust staffing levels, the manager receives delegation without empowerment. By assigning a sales director the objective of increasing revenue by 10% while their teams are understaffed, and without granting them the authority to hire additional salespeople, management effectively programs their failure—unless management later agrees to provide additional resources. This approach sneakily establishes a relationship of subordination, where the sales director becomes inherently subject to management's discretionary power.

To deliver expected results, the sales director depends entirely on management's benevolent willingness to grant necessary resources. This creates a position of dependency where success is contingent not on the director's capabilities or efforts, but on management's magnanimous allocation of resources.

This discreet but highly effective mechanism of subordination is experienced daily by millions of employees. It represents a subtle yet powerful form of organizational control, where formal responsibility exists without true authority, creating a persistent state of dependency on higher management's discretionary decisions. The result is a system where formal delegation masks continued centralized control, creating an illusion of autonomy while maintaining traditional power structures. Real empowerment requires aligning responsibility, authority, and resource control at the same organizational level.

In Practice

When examined through the lens of caring, it becomes evident that demanding results from employees without granting them authority over the means of achieving these results represents a form of organizational constraint that lacks fundamental consideration for human dignity. True empowerment, which involves sharing decision-making power, inherently demonstrates both care and trust in employees' capabilities.

Granting decision-making authority creates freedom of action, which naturally reduces stress levels among employees. This stress reduction represents another manifestation of organizational care. Furthermore, empowerment serves as a catalyst for personal development, offering opportunities for growth and self-actualization.

The relationship between empowerment and caring operates on multiple levels:

- The act of sharing decision-making power demonstrates respect for individual judgment and capability
- The freedom to choose methods and approaches allows for personal expression and creativity
- The reduction in supervisory constraints diminishes workplace anxiety and pressure
- The opportunity for autonomous decision-making facilitates learning and professional development

This perspective reveals empowerment not merely as a management technique but as an expression of organizational values that prioritize human well-being and development. When you genuinely empower your employees, you create conditions that support both individual growth and organizational success through reduced stress, increased engagement, and enhanced personal investment in outcomes.

"**In driving, the passenger typically experiences more stress than the driver because the driver maintains control over the situation.**"[5] This powerful observation from Philippe Rodet and Yves Desjacques, drawing from Karasek's model, illustrates how lack of control determines stress levels. This fundamental insight reveals how autonomy directly impacts psychological well-being.

Organizations that resist empowerment pay a significant price. Employees who are not trusted naturally demonstrate reduced engagement, which inevitably results in diminished productivity and profitability. The benefits of empowerment appear clear and multiple, making its limited implementation in organizations particularly puzzling.

The root cause of this resistance seems to lie in management's apprehension of losing power and/or employees acting independently without close supervision. These fears, however, reveal a more fundamental organizational failure: inadequate recruitment and selection processes. When managers hesitate to grant decision-making authority, they implicitly acknowledge having hired individuals whom they do not trust sufficiently to make autonomous decisions.

This situation creates a self-perpetuating cycle: management hires without sufficient attention to autonomy and decision-making capabilities. This leads to a lack of trust in employees' judgment. The resulting close supervision and limited autonomy create stress and disengagement. Reduced performance then appears to justify the initial lack of trust.

The solution requires addressing of the root cause by:

- Recruiting individuals with demonstrated capacity for autonomous decision making
- Selecting for both technical competence and judgment capabilities
- Building organizational cultures that nurture and reward initiative
- Developing trust-based management practices that support empowerment

This analysis suggests that the limited implementation of empowerment does not reflect its lack of value but rather systemic failures in organizational hiring and management practices. The inconsistency in this approach to trust becomes strikingly apparent when examining your daily life. You regularly place extraordinary trust in complete strangers for matters of life and death:

- You entrust your life to unknown taxi drivers and airline pilots
- You put your health in the hands of anonymous cooks and food producers
- You place your children's safety with daycare workers and nannies you barely know
- You trust hotel staff with your basic hygiene needs
- You rely on medical professionals without verifying their credentials
- You depend on guides to ensure your survival in challenging sports adventures

---

[5] Philippe Rodet and Yves Desjacques, "*Le Management bienveillant*," Eyrolles, 2017.

In each of these scenarios, you extend profound trust to individuals whose qualifications were verified by unknown third parties, through processes you have never scrutinized. You accept these risks without hesitation, often placing your life or that of your loved ones in their hands.

This trust paradox becomes even more striking when contrasted with organizational behavior: managers often hesitate to empower employees whom they personally selected through careful recruitment processes, extensive interviews, and thorough background checks. These are individuals whose capabilities have been directly assessed, whose references have been verified, and whose performance can be monitored daily.

The logical inconsistency is clear: if you readily trust unknown individuals with life-critical responsibilities based on indirect verification of their competence, how can you justify withholding trust from employees you have personally vetted? This comparison reveals the irrationality of excessive control in organizational settings. The same managers who would not think twice about trusting a stranger as a pilot might struggle to delegate less critical decision-making authority to their carefully selected team members.

I hope that this realization will challenge you to reconsider your management practices. If you can extend such profound trust in your personal life, you should be even more capable of trusting those you have deliberately chosen to join your organization. The alternative suggests either a fundamental flaw in your recruitment processes or an irrational bias against empowerment that requires serious examination.

If you cannot effectively recruit trustworthy individuals, two critical questions emerge that demand honest self-reflection. First, how can you expect to be considered trustworthy by your staff when your recruitment decisions demonstrate poor judgment? Staff members naturally observe and evaluate these choices, and failed recruitment decisions inevitably undermine their confidence in your leadership judgment. Second, and perhaps more fundamentally, if you lack the ability to identify and select trustworthy individuals for your organization, are you truly qualified for a leadership position?

Trust in professional relationships, like any human connection, carries inherent risks of disappointment. Yet my experience demonstrates that the benefits far outweigh these occasional setbacks. By extending trust to carefully selected colleagues, I created a simpler, more rewarding work environment. Once clear objectives and Engaged Team Charters were established, micromanagement became unnecessary, freeing everyone to focus on achieving results in their own way. It has always worked very well for me.

The persistent resistance to flexible work arrangements particularly illustrates this trust deficit in management. The insistence on physical presence and rigid schedules, when work could be effectively performed elsewhere, reveals a fundamental lack of trust (which may be the result of recruiting untrustworthy employees). I am convinced that this controlling approach predictably results in diminished employee engagement and reduced productivity.

This situation creates a self-reinforcing cycle:

- Management demonstrates distrust through rigid control measures
- Employees perceive this lack of trust and respond with decreased engagement
- Decreased engagement leads to lower performance
- Lower performance appears to justify increased control
- Increased control further diminishes trust and engagement

The irony lies in how this controlling approach often creates the very problems that it seeks to prevent. By refusing to trust employees with flexibility, organizations:

- Limit their access to talent that demands flexible arrangements
- Reduce employee satisfaction and well-being
- Increase unnecessary overhead costs for controlling purposes
- Miss opportunities for improved productivity through optimized employee engagement
- Create artificial barriers to performance

This management stance reflects a deeper organizational dysfunction— either a fundamental failure in recruitment practices or an ingrained cultural mistrust that undermines both individual and organizational potential. The solution requires not just changing policies but transforming the underlying mindset about trust and control in the workplace.

The logic of empowerment flows naturally through a sequence of interconnected benefits: empowerment builds on trust, which in turn elevates engagement. This engagement drives spontaneous performance, thereby reducing the need for leadership intervention. As intervention decreases, leaders gain space for strategic focus, ultimately leading to reduced stress and increased satisfaction for all involved.

Although this virtuous circle offers compelling benefits, successful implementation requires three key elements. First, careful selection of trustworthy team members forms the foundation. Second, establishing clear frameworks and expectations through Engaged Team Charters provides necessary safeguarding. Third, maintaining balanced autonomy with regular check-ins ensures accountability without micromanagement.

In Practice

Denying employees decision-making freedom not only contradicts empowerment principles but fundamentally signals distrust in their judgment capabilities. When a collaborator acknowledges their limitations in certain areas, this creates no conflict. However, problems arise when competent employees are denied decision-making authority they believe that they deserve. They inevitably conclude that you fail to recognize their capabilities, revealing your own lack of judgment. This realization leads to a critical question: why should they trust a leader who lacks the discernment to recognize and trust demonstrated competence?

However, empowerment cannot mean unlimited trust in every employee in all situations. The solution lies in clearly defining the boundaries of decision-making authority. The Engaged Team Charter serves this purpose by establishing clear rules that prevent empowerment from becoming unmanageable. Beyond these general principles, specific limitations may need to be defined for particular missions, circumstances or responsibilities.

The process of setting these boundaries proves most effective when done collaboratively rather than through unilateral managerial decree. When employees participate in defining the scope and limitations of their authority, they develop a deeper understanding of the rationale behind these boundaries and are more likely to respect them. This collaborative approach transforms limitations from imposed restrictions into mutually agreed guidelines, fostering both trust and responsibility.

This balanced approach ensures that empowerment remains both meaningful and manageable, creating a framework where trust can flourish within appropriate boundaries. It acknowledges that true empowerment requires not just the granting of authority but also the mutual understanding of its scope and limits.

Lever 13 • Boost Your Employees' Resilience and Self-Confidence

The effectiveness of empowerment depends heavily on employee resilience— the capacity to both recover from setbacks and capitalize on opportunities. Having resilient employees provides you with psychological security, knowing that your teams can handle adversity and seize positive circumstances. Conversely, doubting collaborator resilience creates perpetual anxiety about their responses to challenges and their ability to recognize opportunities.

Self-confidence forms an essential foundation for resilience, particularly confidence in one's ability to overcome difficulties and bounce back from failure. Therefore, building employees' confidence in their capabilities and potential serves your interests by enabling innovative thinking and reducing paralysis from fear of mistakes.

Yet paradoxically, many organizations and managers unconsciously undermine employee confidence through various destructive practices, including:

- Excessive focus on minor errors
- Stigmatization of failures
- Undervaluation of existing skills
- Disproportionate emphasis on weaknesses or "development areas"
- Ostentatious displays of superior knowledge or experience
- Subtle or overt criticism, humiliation, and failure to acknowledge achievements

These confidence-eroding behaviors, although allowing managers to assert dominance and reinforce hierarchical submission, ultimately prove self-defeating. By diminishing employee self-confidence, managers create tension and disengage their teams. This approach not only lacks basic fairness and caring but also demonstrates poor strategic judgment—leaders effectively sabotage their own success by suppressing the very qualities that would make their teams more effective and their own roles easier.

The irony lies in how these controlling behaviors, intended to maintain managerial authority, actually weaken organizational capability and increase leadership burden. Supporting collaborator confidence and resilience, rather than undermining them, serves both humanitarian and practical leadership goals.

In Practice

Shifting focus from employee weaknesses to actively cultivating their self-confidence and resilience creates stronger organizations. Rather than dwelling on deficiencies, leaders should consistently seek opportunities to build these essential qualities in their teams.

Multiple tools exist for developing staff resilience, extending beyond basic resilience-building techniques. Professional development programs, such as the AgilityBooster/MicroMBA,[6] implemented across various companies and health care institutions, demonstrate how executive training can effectively enhance collaborator resilience and agility. These programs challenge participants to function as true intrapreneurs on real projects, pushing them to:

- Discover and utilize previously untapped personal potential
- Move beyond traditional project execution skills
- Step outside their comfort zones
- Develop healthy relationships with failure
- Face authentic challenges that build both resilience and self-confidence

Strengths-based leadership workshops teaching people how to exploit their strengths as described in lever 16 provide another powerful tool for increasing staff self-confidence. Managers who implement these workshops consistently report improvements in:

- Team resilience levels
- Trust between management and staff
- Collaborator engagement
- Overall team performance

---

[6] www.MicroMBA.net

The key lies in creating structured opportunities for employees to stretch their capabilities while maintaining appropriate support. This approach helps team members to discover their potential through practical experience rather than theoretical instruction. When employees successfully navigate real challenges, they develop lasting confidence in their abilities and greater resilience in facing future obstacles.

Lever 14 • Support Your Employees and Make Yourself Available

Employees naturally look to their manager for support and encouragement. They expect a multifaceted guide who can serve as advisor, mentor, coach, and consultant—someone reliable during challenging times. Although this supportive role can be deeply satisfying for managers, it contains a hidden trap.

The danger lies in how support is provided. When managers showcase their expertise to solve problems, they risk creating an unintended dynamic: each display of superior knowledge can subtly diminish their employees' self-confidence and reinforce dependency. This approach, though well-intentioned, may not actually reflect caring leadership.

Two contrasting approaches to support emerge. Supporting others by constantly demonstrating your superior competence can overshadow and disempower your employees. When you take every opportunity to shine, you may boost your own self-confidence at the expense of your employees' confidence. Needless to say, this is not a caring approach. In contrast, supporting others by valuing and developing your employees' own capabilities builds their confidence and independence. This approach requires more patience and restraint, but it creates a really lasting positive impact. It embodies caring leadership by fostering growth and autonomy rather than dependency.

Leaders must consistently ask themselves whether their support style effectively empowers their employees. The goal should be to develop employees who become increasingly capable and independent, rather than maintaining a dynamic of dependence on the leader's knowledge.

The key to fair and caring support lies in perspective-taking: will your employees perceive that you are building their capability and confidence or merely showcasing your expertise? Although this self-reflection is challenging and subject to personal biases, awareness of these dynamics is crucial for providing truly supportive leadership. It is half the battle.

Support requires genuine availability—a precious and finite resource. Just claiming to be available is not enough; you must actively make time for your colleagues. As time cannot be replaced or increased, dedicating it to others represents a genuine act of caring.

Limited availability signals a lack of caring and support. When employees must chase their manager between appointments, it communicates that they are not a priority. This dynamic undermines the supportive relationship essential for effective leadership.

You must intentionally manage your schedule to ensure that you are available. Just as students need time and encouragement from teachers, employees require consistent support and availability from their managers.

Availability is a key component of the concept of "Servant leadership,"[7] which is or has been very popular. Although this widely discussed concept emphasizes the leader's role in supporting collaborator success, I would like to point out that its implementation does not automatically equate to caring leadership. A leader can provide service while primarily pursuing their own objectives, making employees instruments for personal success. This utilitarian approach, focused on the leader's goals rather than genuine employee well-being, falls short of true caring leadership.

The distinction lies in intention and authenticity. True caring leadership prioritizes employees' development and well-being, and not only as a means of achieving the leader's objectives. This essential difference highlights the potential gap between appearance and reality in leadership styles. Authentic caring leadership requires genuine commitment to employee growth and well-being, transcending purely strategic considerations.

Another often underutilized component is support during effort. In a results-oriented society, which is not a bad thing in itself, the temptation is to congratulate only when the result has been achieved. By analogy, the basketball coach should only express his support at the end of the match, when the result is known...

The good coach does not wait until the end of the match. He is out on the pitch, cheering his players on throughout the match, and even more so during difficult phases.

Employees, like athletes, need support and recognition during their efforts, not just at the moment of achievement. This requires:

• Maintaining close proximity to understand ongoing challenges
• Developing empathy to recognize when support is most needed
• Providing timely encouragement during difficult phases
• Being present and engaged throughout the process

Without maintaining proximity, you risk missing critical moments when support is most impactful. The ability to recognize and respond to these moments depends on staying connected with your team members' experiences and challenges throughout their journey.

---

[7] https://en.wikipedia.org/wiki/Servant_leadership

Testimony of Clémence, Project Manager

"The leader I am going to introduce in these few lines is my former N+2. Until 1 January 2014, he was in charge of a team of 12 people. My N+1 managed three people in this team (including me). Since then, my N+1 is still the same, but we have changed N+2 and manager. However, I still work directly for 'my leader' on specific projects. My leader still manages seven people directly and three indirectly (a secretary, a project manager from my team, and myself).

Talking to my former colleagues not so long ago, they told me about an off-site conflict resolution seminar, during which everyone was both able and obliged to say what was bothering them and what they would like to see changed. Everyone was amazed at the effectiveness of the day, which helped to resolve all tensions. This is an example of the various 'peri-professional' actions that my leader puts in place. This kind of approach shows that the leader can analyze his team and its dysfunctions, and that his objective is to prevent occasional 'assholes' from becoming certified ones! This was not explicitly the case when he was still managing my N+1...

On the other hand, my leader takes an interest in others and shows empathy for his colleagues. He is concerned that they maintain a good work–life balance and is alert to the little symptoms that might be brewing a future burnout. He once said to me directly, 'Are you sure you are going to be all right, you are not going to burn out? We can talk about it.' Admittedly, this may not be the most academic approach to the subject, but it aligns with my working style. Here again, he demonstrates a certain emotional intelligence in his relationships.

Professionally, he knows how to defend our projects and get involved, even in difficult times. I see him as a 'family man' rather than an 'executive' manager. Even more so as he is also demanding, whether in terms of the quality of his work or meeting deadlines.

He vigorously fosters group spirit, regularly organizing meals for the whole team, seminars, or team-building sessions.

But unlike many managers, his leadership qualities lie in his ability to allow himself to be challenged and to encourage constructive confrontation. Even if the final decision rests with him, he is very open to other points of view and readily incorporates the ideas of others. Honestly, I think this is such a rare quality that it is almost to his disadvantage, as I sometimes get the impression that he is seen by his peers as 'weak,' even though he is collaborative. Caring leadership is not yet a religion in my company!

In concrete terms, without going into all the tools used consciously or unconsciously by my leader, it is clear that he orients his management-leadership around the three imperatives of collective success, fairness, and caring, the latter being the breeding ground for motivation and fulfillment."

In Practice

Support also means standing up for your employees if they are attacked or victims of injustice or circumstance. Your employees count on you to stand up for them. If they realize that you have not defended them, they will never be able to trust you again.

A strong indicator that you have defended your team members lies in the fact that you have put yourself personally at risk. If you have taken a personal risk, it means that you have thrown yourself into the fray and engaged in the defense process. Otherwise, it means that you are only scratching the surface, never truly getting your feet wet. If your team members recognize that you have put yourself at risk to defend them, they will owe you a debt of gratitude.

As a manager, you will be judged on your level of personal involvement, both in defending your direct reports and in supporting them in their daily work.

Essential questions for self-reflection include:

- Do your direct reports feel supported? It is not your opinion as a manager that counts, but the perception of your employees
- How much time do you spend with your direct reports, and is it enough for them?
- Have you taken advantage of every opportunity to develop your direct reports?

Practical implementation might include scheduling regular one-on-one meetings with each team member to address their questions and help them to settle any outstanding issues. The frequency of these meetings, which also serve as opportunities for personal development, should be adjusted according to individual circumstances. Remember that when you set aside time for them in your diary, it is proof that they exist for you. It is an act of recognition.

As with trust, the only real question when it comes to support is your employees' perception. Even if you think you are supporting them, but they do not see it that way, you are living in an illusion. To get it right, you should occasionally ask them the questions suggested above.

Lever 15 • Develop Your Employees' Employability

There are essentially two ways of training employees: by providing them with the skills that they lack either for the good of the organization or for their own good. In the latter case, the aim is to improve their employability by providing them with the means of developing their skills. The difference between the two lies in the purpose. Who benefits from employee training?

In the first case, training serves the organization's success, and there is nothing caring about it. In the second case, the aim is to help your collaborator to grow and retain their employability, which is a really caring approach. Ideally, there is a third case: training should kill two birds with one stone, achieving both objectives. This is what HR spontaneously mentions, even if it does not always correspond to reality.

The approach makes a meaningful difference. When training is presented to fill gaps during periodic interviews, the message becomes essentially prescriptive ("you should train to acquire that skill that you lack") and primarily serves organizational interests. This approach risks being perceived as a statement of incompetence ("if I'm being trained, it is because I am incompetent"), potentially coupled with a cynical interpretation ("if I am being trained, it is not for me, but because the organization needs these skills"). Under these conditions, the invitation to train is not well-received.

A focus on employability changes everything. When periodic appraisals are aimed at maintaining or improving employability (beyond just the current employer), the collaborator's perception shifts dramatically, and the message is perceived as caring. For example, programs such as AgilityBooster/MicroMBA,[8] which I have managed for over 20 years, succeed because participants join voluntarily, understanding that the learning will benefit their careers. They recognize their employer's caring approach to training, leading to improved retention and a greater investment in their personal development. This benefits both the employee and the company, resulting in more effective employees and innovative projects.

In Practice

Training courses are not the only way of developing employees. Sending your employees elsewhere for training is the easy solution. Your personal involvement in their development is another matter. It is a true testament to your level of caring.

Transform challenges into growth opportunities for your employees. Following the principle, "Give a man a fish, and you feed him for a day. Teach a man to fish, and you feed him for a lifetime," you should guide employee to find solutions rather than providing immediate answers. This approach helps employees to develop problem-solving skills and independence.

Building autonomy and empowerment requires teaching employees to think strategically and access necessary resources. As they become more independent, their reliance on you diminishes, creating more autonomous team members and freeing you up to focus on other priorities.

---

[8]These programs develop participants' professional agility and entrepreneurial capacity by teaching them to identify, thoroughly analyze, sell, and implement a real project within their company, which they themselves have to find, in the context of leaderless teams. Unable to rely on hierarchical authority, they are led to experiment in the field with the tools of Fair and Caring leadership, which is also part of the training program. See www.MicroMBA.net

This practical approach embodies several key principles:
- Learning through real project implementation rather than theoretical exercises
- Developing leadership skills in nonhierarchical contexts
- Building entrepreneurial capabilities within existing organizations
- Applying Fair and Caring leadership principles in actual business situations
- Creating value for both the participant and their organization

The spirit of companionship requires you to prepare employees for excellence, much like a master guiding an apprentice. Employees fortunate enough to be supported in this way will always be grateful to the leader who has passed on to them the keys to excellence. This approach demands pedagogical skills and a conscious effort to resist the temptation of providing quick answers instead of guidance.

Challenge with care, but ensure that challenges remain accessible. Present opportunities that promote growth while avoiding setting your employees up for failure with impossible tasks. Remember to adapt development opportunities to individual aspirations and respect that not everyone shares the same ambitions.

Share comprehensive knowledge beyond just minimal or required technical expertise. This includes understanding of organizational strategy, awareness of power dynamics, and knowledge of influence networks. You must share not only your business expertise and know-how but also the information to which you have access. Without a good understanding of these elements, employees will be handicapped in their careers.

This holistic approach to development requires more effort than traditional training but creates lasting impact on your employees' careers and capabilities. The investment in time and effort demonstrates genuine caring leadership while building a more capable, independent workforce.

Lever 16 • Capitalize on Your Employees' Strengths

The Gallup Institute[9] has shown that capitalizing on your employees' strengths produces significant measurable benefits:

- Individual productivity increases by 6.8%
- Team productivity rises by 12.5%
- Profitability improves by 8.9%
- Engagement levels multiply by a factor of 6
- Staff turnover reduces by 14.9%
- Employees' quality of life improves by 300%

As getting people to compensate for their weaknesses is like getting them to swim against the tide, the underlying idea of strengths-based leadership[10] is that it is more effective, and therefore wiser, to capitalize on their strengths. In fact, it seems that surfing on one's strengths can overcome certain weaknesses. The example of Steve Jobs illustrates this well: there is no shortage of testimonials about his difficult character and the fact that he was not a model of caring. Despite this, he had other qualities that largely outweighed his weaknesses. By surfing on his genius, he eclipsed his shortcomings.

---

[9] J. Asplund and N. Blacksmith, "Strengthening Your Company's Performance," Gallup Business Journal, 2011. https://www.gallup.com/businessjournal/146351/strengthening-company-performance.aspx

[10] www.strengths-leadership.com

Not everyone is Steve Jobs, and not everyone has his genius, but surfing on your strengths is certainly more rewarding than trying to compensate for your weaknesses. It is not a question of giving up the effort to improve certain things that deserve improvement but of allocating your energy more efficiently. As the popular saying goes, "Everyone has genius, but if you judge a fish by its ability to climb trees, it will spend its whole life thinking it is stupid!"[11]

To make the most of this at team level, it is necessary to highlight everyone's strengths and discuss how best to use them within the team. If one of your colleagues has trouble writing elegantly (a weakness), but is very good at statistical analysis, you could ask another colleague who is more at ease with writing to produce the reports, asking the one who is good at mathematics to relieve those who suffer with numbers. That is real teamwork...

Being aware of one's strengths helps to build self-esteem, which is a key component of the sense of personal effectiveness. The latter is itself a key factor in the self-confidence that contributes to performance. Indeed, Philippe Rodet and Yves Desjacques state[12] unequivocally—drawing on the work of Canadian psychologist Albert Bandura—that employees with a strong sense of self-efficacy are more successful than others. They add that "generally speaking, an individual's perception of their abilities is a good predictor of performance." They even admit that increasing feelings of self-efficacy helps to reduce stress levels. Clearly, to maximize performance and reduce stress levels, it is in your best interest to capitalize on the strengths of your employees.

On the other hand, the lack of recognition, reprimands, humiliations, contempt, denigration, derogatory comments, lack of consideration, and all the other behaviors that unfortunately make up the daily routine of many employees, undermine their dignity and are eminently counter-productive. By diminishing employees' sense of self-efficacy, "assholes" (as defined in Robert Sutton's "The No Asshole Rule") clearly sabotage performance.

Developing each team member's sense of personal effectiveness is therefore a non-negotiable duty for you as a manager.

The Defrocked Priest[13]

"Our company was growing, with expanding product lines achieving solid success. During this growth phase, we placed a job advertisement in the local press seeking skilled workers. One day, a tall, elegant man with impeccable speech came to be interviewed. Looking at him, I had to ask, 'Why are you responding to this advertisement? You clearly are not a skilled worker.'

---

[11] This saying is widely attributed to Albert Einstein, but there is no evidence that he actually said or wrote these words.

[12] Philippe Rodet and Yves Desjacques, op. cit.

[13] Excerpt from Freddy Sarfati, "L'Entreprise autrement," L'Harmattan, 2010.

He replied candidly, 'You are right—I am a defrocked priest. I have lived in Latin America and speak seven languages fluently.' Somewhat taken aback, I pressed further, 'And you are interested in a tradesman position?' knowing that this seemed unlikely.

His response was enlightening, 'Well, if you are looking for skilled workers, you must have managers and administrators too. In any company, there are always human problems to solve. You need people who know how to prevent conflicts, communicate effectively, and treat others with consideration. These are skills I possess.'

For the next 20 years, he served as our telephone operator. His approach and communication style profoundly influenced not just our staff, but our entire network of contacts. His cultural sophistication and unfailing courtesy fostered respected relationships throughout our business community. He established a professional tone through his persistent attention to others and conciliatory demeanor.

Blessed with an exceptional memory and keen awareness of organizational dynamics, he reliably tracked everyone's appointments, meetings, customer visits, and supplier interactions—all without using an electronic calendar. From his position at the center of information flow, he became an indispensable 'liaison hub' for the entire organization."

This inspiring story shows that the most valuable skills are not always the ones listed in the job description. Although the company was looking for traditional skilled workers, it found someone whose soft skills created unprecedented value. The defrocked priest brought unique qualities that transformed what might have been seen as a simple telephone operator position into a central organizational hub.

In Practice

Effectively implementing strengths-based leadership begins with an accurate assessment of employees own strengths—a task more challenging than most realize. Although people often think that they understand their strengths well, research shows that this self-awareness is frequently incomplete or inaccurate. Tools such as Gallup's Strengths-finder questionnaire can help to reveal these hidden or misunderstood capabilities.

However, merely identifying strengths is insufficient. The approach gains significant power when you create an environment that actively nurtures strength development across your team. Patricia Torres's strengths-based leadership methodology,[14] grounded in positive psychology and coaching principles,

---

[14] See www.strengths-leadership.com

demonstrates this comprehensive approach. Her method helps leaders not only to identify their own strengths but also to activate those of team members, enhancing both self-awareness and understanding of others—key components of emotional intelligence.

Although traditional profiling methods primarily identify individual preferences and characteristics, strengths-based leadership takes a more dynamic and practical approach. Rather than just cataloguing or outlining differences, it focuses on actively leveraging each person's unique capabilities for collective success.

The real power of strengths-based leadership lies in its action orientation. Instead of stopping at identification, it provides a framework for maximizing each team member's natural talents—working with the "raw material" present in your team, regardless of their psychological profiles. This approach transforms static profiling into dynamic development.

By actively seeking and developing the best in each person, you demonstrate genuine caring while achieving practical results.

This dual benefit—improving both performance and engagement—makes strengths-based leadership particularly valuable in modern organizations. This positive focus not only enhances performance but also builds stronger, more resilient workplace relationships. Regardless of team members' psychological profiles, this approach works to optimize available talents.

Lever 17 • Prevent Demotivation of Your Employees

Most theories explaining how to motivate others leave much to be desired. After years of experience, I remain unconvinced by any of them. Sustainable motivation cannot be manufactured through manipulation. True, lasting motivation must come from within—it is intrinsic and endogenous. This internal drive proves far more powerful than any external influence. Your role as a manager is not to create motivation, but to nurture and channel what already exists within your employees.

This perspective challenges the myth of the all-powerful, charismatic leader who supposedly transforms their workforce through rousing speeches. Although such scenarios might exist during crises, I have rarely witnessed them in everyday business settings. Even if not entirely mythical, this approach remains too exceptional to serve as a practical management model for typical leaders. Although the leadership insights from figures such as Churchill, Gandhi, Mao, or Martin Luther King fascinate us, they rarely translate effectively to ordinary organizational management.

Interestingly, employee motivation[15] often peaks at a specific moment: the evening before their first day at work. Future employees envision the dawn of a new life, imagining their first step on the path to success. They feel energized, eager to demonstrate their capabilities and potential.

---

[15] This refers not to motivation for a job that merely pays the rent, but to motivation for a position where an employee seeks growth and self-realization.

Unfortunately, this initial enthusiasm often diminishes relatively quickly. New employees discover that their path to success differs from their expectations. The workplace reality—its rules, culture, and dynamics—frequently clashes with their hopes and assumptions. As they encounter or observe disappointing situations, their motivation inevitably declines.

In Practice

This loss of motivation inevitably leads to decreased engagement levels. To maximize engagement, you should prevent what I have just described from occurring. By maintaining the high level of motivation that existed the evening before their first day, you will never need to wonder how to motivate your teams.

Maintaining existing motivation is far easier than trying to recover it after it has been lost. When employees become less motivated, they are left with the bitter taste of frustration—a feeling that is extremely difficult to eliminate. You may need to expend enormous effort just to lessen this bitterness, knowing that some residual effects will likely persist despite your best efforts.

By preventing individual demotivation, you can sustain your employees' highest level of engagement. To do this, you must "simply" eliminate demotivating factors. Begin by identifying these factors and taking the necessary steps to mitigate or at least minimize their impact.

Leveraging intrinsic motivation helps you to combat one of the workplace's most insidious enemies: meaningless work. When employees find no purpose in their tasks, they succumb to various forms of disengagement. The numbers paint a stark picture: 26% of employees[16] suffer from bore-out,[17] 44% experience brown-out,[18] and 12%[19] face burnout.[20] This could mean that 82% of your workforce might be significantly underperforming. Even more concerning, the remaining 18%—those not affected by these syndromes—are not necessarily engaged.

---

[16] www.kintsu.fr/index.php/2019/02/12/sante-mentale/3. "Quand le travail n'a plus de sens."

[17] Bore-out is a psychological disorder caused by a lack of meaningful work, leading to severe boredom and eventual depression. Unlike burnout from overwork, bore-out stems from being underutilized or performing tasks perceived as pointless. https://en.wikipedia.org/wiki/Boreout

[18] Brown-out describes a state of corporate depression where employees maintain functionality but have lost their sense of purpose and motivation, operating well below their potential.

[19] https://www.lemonde.fr/economie/article/2014/01/22/plus-de-3-millions-de-francais-au-bord-du-burn-out_4352438_3234.html

[20] Burnout is a state of physical and emotional exhaustion resulting from prolonged stress and overwork, characterized by cynicism, detachment, and a sense of ineffectiveness.

Testimony of Romane, Head Pastry Chef

"This story takes place in a five-star hotel, where I led a pastry team of about ten people. The pastry assistant in question was a young man around 19–20 years old. I had struggled with him, as he sometimes arrived late to work and lacked precision in executing his assigned tasks.

One Sunday evening, only two of us were scheduled as the service was usually quiet. That night, the restaurant was unexpectedly busy, but with good organization, everything should have run smoothly.

The critical moment came when most tables ordered desserts simultaneously, entering what we call '*le coup de feu*' (the rush hour). The assistant was working well, and we were sending out desserts at a good pace.

Then came an order for two passion fruit soufflés with coconut ice cream. The soufflés require exactly 8 min of baking, not a second more, and must reach the guests immediately to maintain their perfect rise, just as they come out of the oven. This demands precise coordination between the pastry kitchen and dining room staff.

With the soufflés in the oven, we continued preparing other desserts. When the timer rang, the assistant said, 'I've got this!' Ten seconds later, I heard a sliding sound... As I turned around, I watched the baking tray with both soufflés slip across the marble counter, crash into the waiting plates, and everything ended up on the floor in a cacophony of broken china and metal!

The server, who was waiting to serve the desserts, rushed to inform the dining room manager. My assistant turned pale, but instead of exploding—as everyone might have expected—I calmly gave him step-by-step instructions to make again the preparation while continuing to handle the mounting dessert orders. I kept watching him from the corner of my eye, providing the next instruction as he completed each step. Once the new soufflés were in the oven, I asked him to resume preparing other desserts.

After the service ended, the assistant apologized for his clumsiness and thanked me for not yelling and for calmly guiding him through re-making the soufflés. I explained that shouting would have only increased his stress to the point where he could not understand instructions—exactly what we did not need in such an urgent situation. I reminded him that pastry-making demands precision in even the most basic movements.

A few weeks later, I noticed that he started arriving on time and showed much more concentration in his work.

Had this incident opened his eyes? Or did he feel indebted?"

The most significant demotivating factor is the gap between new employees' expectations and the actual culture that they discover. To substantially reduce this gap, present the Engaged Team Charter of Chap. 5 to candidates before they accept the position. Reviewing this charter allows them to understand what they are getting into—in other words, know the rules of the game before stepping onto the field—and adjust their expectations accordingly. By minimizing the disconnect between expectations and reality, you significantly reduce the risk of demotivation.

This approach only works effectively when the Engaged Team Charter is practiced, not just written. The manager's responsibility to enforce it is therefore crucial. If the charter's rules of the game are not respected, the manager automatically loses credibility whereas their employees' engagement levels drop substantially. The inevitable result is, of course, decreased team performance.

Lever 18 • No Corporate Double-Speak

Corporate double-speak is a disease that destroys managers' credibility. It attempts to dodge uncomfortable topics by pretending to address them while muddying the waters. The problem is that... your audience is not buying it. They know when you are feeding them a line instead of telling the truth.

Your audience is not just frustrated—they feel disrespected, sensing that their intelligence is being underestimated. Using corporate double-speak insults their intelligence and assumes that they will not be smart enough to see through your smoke and mirrors. Although a few might not catch on, they would have to be remarkably dim—which does not reflect well on your hiring decisions or team selection.

As most of your employees are plenty sharp enough to spot these verbal gymnastics, using corporate double-speak comes across as pure arrogance. It shows that you believe that you can pull the wool over their eyes. This approach never generates engagement—quite the opposite. In many cases, managers who rely on double-speak are basically shooting themselves in the foot.

In Practice

Encourage your employees to communicate without fear. Create a psychologically safe environment where speaking up about corporate jargon and convoluted language is welcomed, not punished. This enables anyone who perceives—or believes that they perceive—the use of corporate double-speak to bring it to the attention of the person using it.

When providing such feedback, follow the principles of caring feedback: be specific, timely, and solution focused. For example, instead of saying "You are using too much corporate speak," try "When you mentioned 'Leveraging synergies to optimize cross-functional deliverables,' I found it difficult to understand the concrete actions needed. Could we discuss this in simpler terms, like what exactly needs to be done and by whom?" This constructive approach prevents the buildup of frustrations while maintaining professional relationships.

3.6   Is the Leader Up to the Task?

Given the numerous behaviors expected of a leader, it is evident that the bar is set high and not everyone can reach it. True wisdom lies in recognizing one's limitations and avoiding the path to failure. Each manager must evaluate their capacity to meet their employees' expectations.

If you realize that you cannot meet these expectations, it is better to redirect your career toward a path that does not require the same qualities. This may mean taking on a technical expert role that does not involve managing people and thus eliminates the need to maximize their engagement levels.

There is no shame in focusing on what you do well rather than forcing yourself into a leadership role when the expected behaviors do not align with your natural tendencies. This choice will benefit both your well-being and that of your colleagues. Do not underestimate the impact on your health of being surrounded by employees who do not want to follow you but are forced to do so. Even if you do not consciously realize it, your subconscious knows and will manifest its disapproval in one way or another. This can result in discomfort or health issues whose origins may be difficult to identify. Is it worth the struggle? I doubt it.

The cost to your physical and mental well-being, combined with the negative impact on your team, suggests that pursuing a leadership role when it does not align with your natural capabilities may be more harmful than beneficial.

In Practice

To determine whether you maintain your employees' trust and thus a semblance of credibility, you should conduct a self-assessment covering all expected behaviors.

To avoid deceiving yourself with unfounded beliefs or the illusion that you are well-suited to your role, you should supplement your self-assessment by inviting your employees to evaluate you on each expected behavior. To ensure that employees can express themselves freely and without fear of retaliation, it is advisable to offer them the option to respond anonymously, as is possible with the freemium software EazyMirror. The value of this evaluation lies in its ability to reveal your followers' true perceptions helping you to avoid the pitfalls of self-delusion.

It will then be up to you to draw the necessary conclusions about your ability to lead your team.

3.7   Visual Summary: Fair and Caring Leadership Behaviors

Figure 3.1 provides a visual summary of the Fair and Caring Leadership levers associated with expected leader behaviors

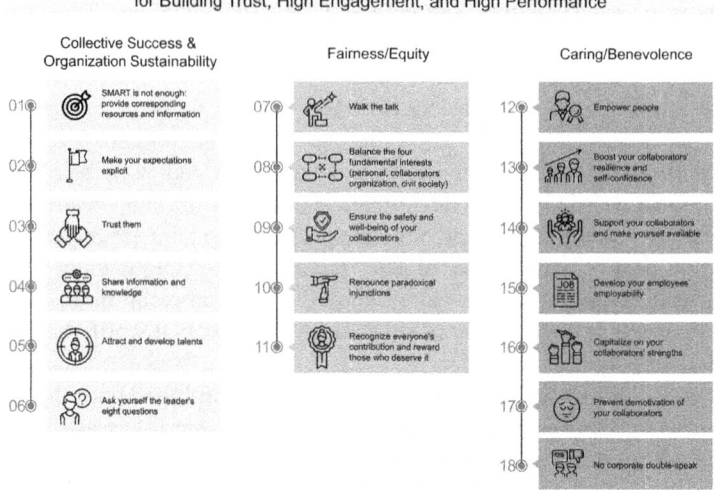

Fig. 3.1 Summary of Fair and Caring Leadership levers linked to expected leader behaviors

Your Leadership Traits

4

4.1 Traits That Foster Engagement

Leadership remains an inexhaustible—and far from exhausted—source of analysis for decoding its secrets. A vast body of research and literature is devoted to leadership qualities and personality traits. There is no need to attempt a synthesis here, as others have done—and continue to do this—far more comprehensively than I could. However, I believe it is important to highlight several qualities and traits which, in my experience, foster engagement through fair and caring leadership. Although this list is not exhaustive, and not all qualities carry equal weight, it should be substantial enough to inspire and energize those who aspire to be fair and caring leaders.

It is essential to keep in mind that an insufficient level in any of these traits represents a handicap for anyone hoping to inspire their employees to fully invest themselves. The more qualities you lack, the more each deficiency will weigh you down and prevent you from becoming a leader who generates engagement. This is not an invitation to throw in the towel but rather a call to become aware of areas that require improvement. Conversely, your well-developed qualities will serve as strengths upon which you can capitalize.

Just as everyone cannot be a good skilled athlete, leadership is not suited to everyone. Those who aspire to it must either possess or be willing to develop certain qualities. Knowing one's limitations is itself a central quality. Becoming a doctor requires certain qualities and competencies. Someone who lacks these but insists on practicing would be a public danger. The same applies to leaders: their incompetence in leadership will cause suffering to those under their responsibility. The psychological pain inflicted by an ill-suited leader is as serious as the physical pain caused by an incompetent doctor.

"Introduction and Warnings" for this book are available in Front matter and "Epilogue" and "Complete Framework for Building Trust, High Engagement, and High Performance" are available in Back matter. Readers can download them free from https://doi.org/10.1007/978-3-032-05172-1.

R. H Cohen, *Driving Employee Engagement*, Management for Professionals, https://doi.org/10.1007/978-3-032-05172-1_4

In Practice

To facilitate individual reflection, the summary table, downloadable from www.driving-engagement.com/download, includes a self-assessment column where you are invited to evaluate your performance on a scale of 0–4. The meaning of each level on this scale is as follows:

0 indicates that you do not possess this trait at all
1 indicates a poor level
2 indicates a level better than 1, but still insufficient
3 indicates a good level that can still be improved (a good level is higher than merely sufficient)
4 indicates a level of excellence requiring no improvement

The advantage of this whole-number scale is that it offers no middle or merely 'sufficient' level. For organizations striving for excellence, anything below 3 is clearly too weak to be acceptable. Those pursuing excellence will view level 3 as an invitation to do even better. Those with more modest goals may find level 3 acceptable.

This self-assessment serves as a mirror, reflecting your aptitude to be a fair and caring leader and, more importantly, allows you to recognize what you can personally do to improve your leadership, in addition to all previously discussed elements. Furthermore, thanks to this table that renders critical personality traits somehow measurable, you can evaluate your own evolution over time.

This approach is not without flaws: it depends on your beliefs. The scores you assign yourself merely express your opinion. They are naturally subjective and likely biased. As the perception of your team members and those around you probably reflects your personality traits more accurately, you can simply ask them to anonymously rate each of your traits for a much more realistic assessment.[1]

4.2   Your Personality Traits for Leading to Collective Success

Lever 19 • Be a Source of Inspiration

Anyone capable of inspiring their employees naturally achieves a high level of engagement, which translates into better performance. The challenge lies in... inspiring.

Charisma, often defined as the ability to attract and influence others, frequently comes up in leadership discussions. Charisma presents two challenges: first, possessing it—which is not universal—and second, sustaining it. Furthermore, as it is not easy to define or even determine how much is innate versus acquired,

---

[1] For this purpose, you can use www.EazyMirror.com or equivalent to customize the 360 survey for what you want to investigate.

I am not convinced that charisma is a sufficient parameter. It contains an element of seduction that has certain merit, but like all forms of seduction, it is difficult to maintain over time. Various tools or even artifices, such as public-speaking skills, can contribute to charisma, but for it to be sustainable, trust must be maintained. Once trust erodes, charisma collapses.

Rather than focusing on charisma, I prefer to concentrate on the ability to inspire. Although charisma can certainly contribute to this ability, it is not a prerequisite. I have known leaders who had little charisma but were deeply inspiring to their teams. Having also met highly charismatic individuals who failed to inspire over the long term, I conclude that although charisma is beneficial, being inspirational is even more effective.

The most tempting solution is to develop your professional expertise: the more you excel through your knowledge and know-how, the more others will admire you and, incidentally, depend on you. This strategy is gratifying and makes you indispensable. However, it does not promote collective performance, which would be much better if this knowledge were shared across your team. If the entire team possessed your level of expertise, their performance would undoubtedly be even higher.

I have serious doubts about professional expertise being a sufficient source of inspiration to genuinely generate sustained engagement. I have seen many experts whose knowledge everyone recognized, but who inspired no one. Their employees' engagement levels were sometimes particularly low. Being inspirational requires more than expertise alone.

Depending on circumstances and culture, inspiration can come from a leader's genius, intuition, exemplary behavior, generosity, caring nature, sense of fairness, integrity, resilience, numerical ability, clarity of vision, determination to succeed, and more.

As with trust, it appears extremely difficult to exhaustively identify the parameters that make someone inspirational or not. Moreover, as different things inspire different people, the source of inspiration will be influenced by the target audience.

Unfortunately, I have no universal miracle recipe for being inspirational. I simply encourage everyone to reflect on their context and to consider how their actions and attitudes influence the level of engagement that they generate. By examining these connections, you can better understand what might inspire your employees.

In Practice

To accomplish this, you might look in the mirror and ask yourself questions such as:

"How am I a source of inspiration for my team members or colleagues?"
"Is their level of engagement maximized by what I inspire?"
"What could I do or change to be even more inspiring and increase my teams' level of engagement?"

Beyond self-reflection, you could also pose similar questions to your employees. This should help you to understand the extent to which they find you inspiring and what leads them to think so. You can also try to understand why other leaders are sources of inspiration in your organization or profession.

One element that significantly contributes to inspiration is hope. Gallup has notably shown that leaders who succeed in generating enthusiasm for the future (thus hope) among their employees significantly increase their engagement level: 69% compared with 1% for those who do not perceive this hope.[2]

Lever 20 • Maintain Your Credibility Daily

As it is difficult to expect someone to follow you if you are not credible in their eyes, leader credibility is a prerequisite for leadership. The catch is that, like trust, credibility is tested daily and depends on your ability to do the "right thing" in your employees' eyes. Each misstep that sabotages your credibility is extremely difficult to recover from. As with trust, rebuilding requires considerable efforts, bordering on the impossible.

To avoid this descent into hell, be aware of what can affect your credibility. The list is unfortunately very long, but here are the key categories with examples. Your credibility suffers particularly when:

Core Leadership Values

- You are not caring
- You do not demonstrate fairness
- You lack courage
- You have an oversized ego
- You lack emotional intelligence
- You lack self-confidence

Decision-Making and Strategic Capability

- You fail to make decisions
- You do not anticipate sufficiently
- You lack strategic vision
- You lack clear vision
- You create confusion
- You prioritize processes over purpose

Promise and Delivery

- You do not deliver what you promised
- You underestimate how long work takes
- You let problems accumulate
- You distribute work and efforts poorly
- You micromanage
- You suffer from acute "controlitis"

---

[2] https://news.gallup.com/businessjournal/118315/economic-crisis-leadershipchallenge.aspx

Team Management and Development

- You reward someone who field staff believe does not deserve it
- You promote undeserving people
- You do not defend your employees
- You do not implement governance rules that protect your employees
- You fail to recognize your employees' contributions or effort
- You do not help those in need

Power and Authority Usage

- You must use force or hierarchical power to get what you want
- You divide to manipulate and keep control
- You show favoritism
- You show servile submission to superiors
- You avoid taking responsibility
- You diminish others to elevate yourself

Professional Competence

- You do not know/understand what is happening
- You are not a source of inspiration
- You are part of the problem instead of contributing to the solution
- You tolerate mediocrity
- You do not respect all provisions of the Engaged Team Charter[3]
- People do not want to follow you

Communication and Relationship Management

- You tell people to figure it out when you have given them paradoxical instructions
- You do not do what your employees expect of you
- You do not tolerate the right to make mistakes
- You cover your tracks instead of doing the right thing
- You agree with the last person who spoke
- You do not sanction those who deserve it

I will stop here to avoid depressing you. I hope to have at least made you aware of a very simple fact: credibility, like trust, hangs by a thread. But as there are many scissors that can cut this thread, you must maintain constant vigilance.

Claiming that being a leader is easy and that professional expertise is enough to establish credibility is a misconception. Although expertise contributes to credibility, it is far from sufficient. Many other parameters, unrelated to professional expertise, also play a significant role. The categorized list above testifies to this.

---

[3] See Chap. 5.

This list can serve as a rough self-assessment to give you an idea of your credibility level. If you are a thrill-seeker or appreciate confronting reality, you can certainly survey your employees. They are indeed much better positioned than you to assess how well you avoid each of the above undesirable behaviors.

For a structured self-assessment, consider evaluating yourself in each category using a simple scale (0 to 4):

– Core Leadership Values: rate yourself on each trait (caring, fairness, courage, ego management, emotional intelligence, self-confidence)
– Decision-Making and Strategic Capability: assess your effectiveness in making timely decisions, anticipating issues, and maintaining strategic vision
– Promise and Delivery: evaluate your track record of delivering on commitments and managing work effectively
– Team Management and Development: review your practices in recognition, support, and development of team members
– Power and Authority Usage: reflect on how you exercise authority and handle hierarchical relationships
– Professional Competence: assess your understanding of operations and ability to inspire others
– Communication and Relationship Management: evaluate your effectiveness in clear communication and maintaining professional relationships

There are also tests[4] that measure people's credibility. Not having used them myself, I cannot comment on their relevance, but I do not doubt that the academic world will, if it has not already done so, eventually propose a reliable test for evaluating the credibility of those who want to know where they stand.

Lever 21 • Cultivate Your Resilience

In simplified terms and in a professional context, resilience expresses the ability to face adversity. As it also includes the capacity to bounce back, it goes beyond merely overcoming hardships. It also presupposes the ability to seize opportunities. Indeed, it is through opportunities that you can rebound. Without opportunity, you must wait for the storm to pass, whereas by building a device that harnesses wind power, you can take advantage of the wind that initially disturbed you.

As employees count on their leader to guide and protect them, they expect them not to collapse at the first sign of wind. To feel confident, they must believe in your resilience. A leader who wants to inspire trust must therefore demonstrate resilience and develop it relentlessly.

---

[4] Example: http://www.jamescmccroskey.com/measures/source_credibility.htm

Insofar as it enables opportunities to be seized and obstacles to be overcome, resilience contributes significantly to collective performance. This inner strength thus serves as a guarantee of sustainability.

It is important to recognize that resilience must be established before it is needed. You cannot develop it in the midst of a crisis; it must already be in place when challenges arise. This means that for resilience to be available when you need it, you should take proactive steps to strengthen yours now. If you have not yet started, remember that the ideal time to begin was yesterday, so it is essential to make it a priority today.

As with many other personality traits, the debate between innate and acquired remains open for resilience. Everyone can develop their level of resilience. Various tools are available to measure resilience. As these assessments reveal that resilience stems from numerous parameters, there are many areas for development. Although some components can certainly be improved, others remain beyond your control. You can approach this development process through structured methodologies, such as those offered by specialized providers, but you can also—and should simultaneously—cultivate resilience through real-world field experience.

In Practice

Indeed, each time you step out of your comfort zone, you mobilize resources that strengthen your agility. All challenges are thus opportunities to develop your resilience. When facing adversity, you can collapse, lament, blame fate, or pour your frustration onto others. But you can also view it as an opportunity to test and develop your resilience.

Each time you succeed in overcoming a difficulty, you consolidate your resilience and gain confidence. The greatest enemy of resilience is the fear of failure. If failure is instead experienced as a learning opportunity and treated as such, there is no longer a reason to be afraid. Someone who succeeds in transforming difficulties or even adversity into opportunities is much better prepared for the future.

Two Tales about the Art of Landing on Your Feet
A first tale:
Little Pierre moves to the countryside and invests his savings in a small farm stand to sell local produce. On his first day, a severe storm damages all his fresh inventory, leaving him with a potential loss of 100 euros.

Instead of giving up, Pierre quickly transforms the situation:
"If life gives you damaged produce, make preserves!" he decides.

He turns the bruised apples into homemade apple sauce, the overripe tomatoes into sauce, and the damaged vegetables into soup. He creates attractive labels explaining how his products help to reduce food waste and support sustainable farming.

A month later, his former competitor, the old farmer who runs the big stand down the road, visits Pierre:

"How did you manage after that terrible storm?"

"I turned it into an opportunity! I sold my preserves for 2 euros each and shared the story of reducing food waste. People loved it so much, I made 1000 euros and gained regular customers who now pre-order my preserves!"

"And nobody complained about the damaged produce?"

"Actually, it inspired a community movement. Now, other farmers bring me their imperfect produce, and we share the profits from the preserves. Everyone wins—the farmers, the customers, and the environment!"

And a second less ethical tale:

Little Pierre moves to the countryside and buys a donkey from an old farmer for 100 euros. The farmer agrees to deliver the donkey the next day, but when tomorrow comes:

"Sorry son, but I have bad news: the donkey is dead."

"Well then, give me my money back."

"I can't do that. I've already spent it all..."

"OK then, just bring me the donkey."

"What are you going to do with a dead donkey?"

"I'm going to raffle it off..."

"You can't raffle off a dead donkey!"

"Of course I can. I just won't tell anyone it's dead."

The farmer, in his position, feels he can't really refuse. So he delivers the donkey to little Pierre.

A month later, he comes back to see little Pierre:

"What happened to my dead donkey?"

"I raffled it off. I sold 500 tickets at 2 euros each: that made me... 1000 euros!"

"And nobody complained?"

"Only the guy who won. But I gave him his 2 euros back and he didn't make a fuss!"

Lever 22 • Share Your Passion with Your Employees

Passionate people naturally invest themselves fully in their work. A passionate team will inevitably perform better than one acting merely out of obligation. Having passionate employees translates into higher levels of engagement.

Passion is indeed a highly contagious disease and thus serves as a cost-effective lever for boosting success. With minimal effort, you can stimulate your team's engagement level. This contagion effect works equally well with customers (internal or external). Consider the difference between being served by a genuinely enthusiastic restaurant server versus one who is merely efficient but passionless. For influencing customers, passion proves far more effective than expensive advertising campaigns.

When you do things with passion, time flies by, making work more enjoyable. A DIY enthusiast can spend hours happily tinkering, whereas someone who dislikes it (like me) sees every repair as a burden and waste of time. Passion transforms work into pleasure, naturally leading to increased engagement—a key driver of performance. I am, for instance, passionate about executive education and derive immense satisfaction from every opportunity to help managers to grow and develop. This genuine enthusiasm likely explains why participants in my sessions often tell me that time flies during my presentations.

The crucial question is not whether passion is beneficial—it is. Just as good health enables peak performance, passion enables sustained engagement—whereas brown-out,[5] which affects more than 40% of managers, severely undermines it. The real question is: how does one become passionate?

Authentic passion cannot be faked—it must come from deep conviction. Your team members can easily distinguish between genuine enthusiasm and artificial cheerleading. True passion emerges from your belief in the meaning and value of what you and your team are accomplishing together.

Passion, like motivation or love, cannot be decreed. You cannot simply decide to fall in love or become passionate. Although I do not have a formula for developing passion, I emphasize that insufficient passion comes at a leadership cost through reduced employee engagement. If you aim to be a leader who catalyzes your team's potential, you should seek leadership positions in fields that genuinely interest you personally. Otherwise, you will merely be a good mercenary—which is not shameful but rarely aligns with passionate leadership. As a mercenary, it is important to be honest with yourself about your motivations.

Remember that passion builds resilience. When your team shares your enthusiasm, they are better equipped to overcome challenges and setbacks. A shared sense of purpose and excitement creates stronger bonds and higher engagement, making your team more effective and resilient.

In Practice

As maximizing engagement is a primary function of leadership, passion serves as a key ingredient that costs nothing to utilize. Cooking with passion requires no more time, money, or effort than cooking out of obligation. The impact, however, is dramatically different.

Share Your Vision Through Personal Stories:

Rather than making abstract statements, share specific experiences that ignited your passion. For example, describe a moment when you witnessed your team's work making a real difference, or explain why you believe in your organization's mission. These authentic narratives help team members to connect emotionally with the purpose of their work.

---

[5] See definition of brown-out in footnote 18, p. 74.

Demonstrate Enthusiasm in Daily Actions:
- Show genuine interest in your team's projects by asking thoughtful questions
- Celebrate small wins with sincere excitement
- Remain engaged during challenges, viewing them as opportunities rather than obstacles
- Allocate time for innovation and improvement discussions, showing that you care about growth

Create Opportunities for Others to Connect with Their Passions:
- Help team members to identify aspects of their work that naturally energize them
- Assign projects that align with individual interests and strengths
- Encourage sharing of success stories and positive customer feedback
- Create spaces for team members to propose and lead initiatives that they feel passionate about

Model Continuous Learning and Curiosity:
- Share what you are learning and reading about your field
- Acknowledge knowledge gaps and show enthusiasm for finding answers
- Participate actively in professional development alongside your team
- Demonstrate how challenges can become exciting learning opportunities

Lever 23 • Be Genuinely Authentic

Trust is the ultimate prerequisite for fostering engagement, and employees cannot trust someone who is pretending to be genuine. Those who play a role or pretend to be something that they are not will inevitably be exposed. Employees are perceptive, and inauthenticity will be identified sooner or later. Apart from rare exceptions such as Madoff, who managed to maintain a façade, it is not only difficult but also exhausting over the long term.

True nature always resurfaces! Therefore, you do not have a choice: you must authentically be yourself. It is through being authentic that you become predictable and help your team members to feel secure.

In Practice

Practical Ways to Develop Authentic Leadership:
- Practice self-awareness through regular reflection on your values, strengths, and areas for growth
- Share appropriate personal experiences that demonstrate vulnerability and learning
- Acknowledge mistakes openly and describe how you learned from them
- Express genuine emotions while maintaining professional composure
- Communicate your true thoughts respectfully, even when they differ from those of others
- Make decisions that align with your stated values and principles

Balancing Authenticity with Professional Boundaries:

– Set clear expectations about work relationships while remaining approachable
– Share personal insights relevant to work situations without oversharing private matters
– Express emotions appropriately—showing genuine care while maintaining professional distance
– Establish consistent rules and apply them fairly, explaining your reasoning
– Maintain transparency about business decisions while respecting confidentiality
– Create space for authentic connections within professional parameters

Lever 24 • Have Engaged Followers

Engagement being at the heart of this book, this lever has already been presented in the fundamentals of Chap. 1.

4.3   Your Personality Traits to Support Fairness

In his famous "Art of War,"[6] Sun Tzu writes: "By authority, I mean the general's qualities of wisdom, equity, humanity, courage, and severity." Sun Tzu's genius lies in focusing on the essential. If all leaders maximized these five qualities, the professional world would be vastly different.

Testimony from Sandrine, Sales and Marketing Director
"Caring leadership must eliminate ego and consider employee well-being to help the organization to prosper. I experienced this caring leader in the person of our former general director, Mr. X. One of his main qualities was the empathy and humanity he demonstrated with each of us, at any time of day. A kind word, a joke, a nickname for the lucky ones (!), a helping hand, advice, a reprimand, or even anger from him—everything affected us, and we found it unthinkable to disappoint him. I say 'we' because he had truly achieved unanimity, and we all held great respect and admiration for him.

This admiration he had earned quite easily... He must have read Sun Tzu! Indeed, there is a passage where he cites the example of General Wu Ch'i, who ate and dressed like the humblest of his men, and Mr. X WAS that general."

---

[6] https://en.wikipedia.org/wiki/The_Art_of_War

I believe that these five qualities, as defined by Sun Tzu, are prerequisites for practicing fair and caring leadership. Anyone who does not possess all of them at a highly respectable level has little chance of being recognized as a fair and caring leader.

The Essential Qualities:

- Wisdom is necessary for discernment to accurately understand situations, a prerequisite for fairness. Without discernment, sound judgment and fairness are impossible
- Equity, as the capacity to do what is right, is essential for upholding fairness as an imperative
- Humanity goes hand in hand with caring
- Courage is indispensable for doing what is right and resisting pressures
- Severity, which corresponds to rigor in enforcing agreed-upon rules, is an inevitable component of fairness

For the structure of this book, humanity will be addressed in Chap. 5, whereas the other four qualities constitute the essential content of this Chapter. I have supplemented them with only one additional quality: congruence.

It is interesting to note that the five qualities described by Sun Tzu are ultimately quite similar to the four cardinal virtues identified by Plato: courage, prudence, temperance, and justice. The form changes, but the substance remains similar.

Lever 25 • Demonstrate Fairness

I have already discussed fairness extensively as an imperative, but its importance warrants further development. Aspiring to fairness does not automatically translate into applying and living it. This requires having a sense of fairness—a personal quality that some possess naturally whereas others possess it to a lesser degree or not at all.

Almost everyone aspires to fairness. When I ask the question, "Who does not aspire to fairness?" no one ever raises their hand. However, when I ask managers attending my courses if their leaders should demonstrate more fairness, almost all hands go up (provided that the leaders are not present!).

This reveals a significant gap between targeting fairness and living it, which depends particularly on how each protagonist perceives fairness. Faced with the same situation, two people might have very different perspectives based on:

- Their value systems
- Their worldview
- Their personal history
- The importance they place on emotion
- Other individual filters that influence their perception of fairness

In Practice

The better you know your team members, the better you understand their filters. With this knowledge, you will be able to anticipate how they might interpret what they observe. If you treat employees merely as resources, you will never understand their filters.

This perspective challenges the widespread notion of strictly separating private and professional life. Such separation inevitably leads to not knowing employees as individuals, reducing them to mere resources. Although I am not suggesting mixing private and professional life thoroughly, by taking an interest in your employees as human beings and treating them as such, you will find the "happy medium." Balance is key.

Getting to know people requires opening up to them and sharing something of yourself. You cannot expect to know them without also talking about yourself. Discovery must be mutual and sincere. It is unlikely that employees will be willing to engage and reveal themselves to someone who does not also share something of themselves.

The separation between private and professional life likely stems from an era when work was viewed merely as providing labor power. This concept of "resource" available to the employer, where "renting" a workforce is treated like renting a machine, is fundamentally alienating. As is still the case in some cultures, I emphasize that the vision of work discussed in this book considers it an opportunity for personal fulfillment and self-realization.

Fair and caring leadership is built on co-creation toward a shared purpose that each person embraces and contributes to according to their abilities and skills. The "human resources" logic is therefore the antithesis of fair and caring leadership. This leadership approach is aimed at humanizing relationships between individuals who share the desire to achieve collective success instead of looking at humans as a "resource" or "capital."

The individual remains the same person both at work and outside work:

- Same personality
- Same fears
- Same sense of humor
- Same personal aspirations

Although posture may change with circumstances, personality does not

As your team members are people and not machines or resources, it seems impossible to maintain a strict private/professional life dichotomy. The artificial separation fails to recognize the wholeness of human experience and identity.

Furthermore, equity is not absolute—each person's sense of fairness depends on their personal assessment of what is right. It is essentially a matter of personal judgment, filtered through everyone's unique perspective and experiences. These judgments are processed through the distinct filters that each person possesses:

- Personal values and beliefs as well as the corporate values that have been accepted
- Past experiences
- Cultural background
- Individual circumstances
- Emotional state

Understanding each person's perception of fairness requires knowing the whole person. It seems impossible to fully grasp your team members' filters, aspirations, resistances, and fears if you view them merely as labor resources. You must know and treat them as human beings.

In Practice

As people place significant weight on intention (see Lever 49: apply "fair process"), you must communicate your intentions clearly. Good communication about your intent, justifying what you believe is "the right thing," will help you to avoid many misunderstandings and misinterpretations that could affect your team members' perception of your fairness.

In any case, effective communication requires knowing your audience well, which means understanding their individual filters. This understanding enables you to:

- Frame messages appropriately
- Anticipate potential misinterpretations
- Address concerns proactively
- Build trust through transparent dialogue
- Demonstrate genuine consideration for different perspectives

To ensure that your intent is well understood, I recommend:

- Observing how different team members react to what you say and do to adjust your approach
- Asking for feedback about the intent of what you have said or done, and also how your messages are being received and understood

Demonstrating fairness is challenging but not impossible. Difficulty is never an excuse for inaction. You face only two choices:

- Rise to the challenge—not seeking perfection but making a consistent effort to do your best
- Capitulate—abandoning the ambition to be followed, which means relinquishing all leadership prerogatives

In Practice

As fairness is a matter of perception, the best way to determine how fair you are is to ask your employees to anonymously express their perception of your level of fairness. To this end, you can use the EazyMirror Employee Perceived Fairness Score (EPFS).[7] It asks your employees to what extent they feel that:

1. Their organization (independently of their direct manager) applies fair practices in recruiting, promoting, and treating employees and candidates
2. Their direct manager (as an individual, independently of their superiors or organizational practices) recruits, promotes, and treats team members and candidates fairly
3. Fairness is respected in their working environment

As lack of inclusion or diversity, as well as gender and other forms of discrimination, are all transgressions of fairness, striving to deploy a fair and caring culture should eradicate these issues. Instead of focusing separately on diversity, equality, and inclusion, organizations should simply ensure that everyone is treated fairly. The best way to determine if they achieve this objective is to measure the EPFS, which reveals the extent to which employees consider themselves treated fairly.

Lever 26 • Demonstrate Rigor

Drawing from Sun Tzu's quote, I initially planned to discuss severity, but its current connotation is rather negative owing to people's mental associations. Personally, I appreciate the term "severity" because it strikes the mind and challenges thinking. Because it does not leave people indifferent, severity has the merit of prompting reflection. "Zero tolerance" is another way of expressing Sun Tzu's idea.

Without delving into the etymology or possible evocations of the word, I take the liberty of expressing the intention I see behind it, in Sun Tzu's spirit. The idea is to make no compromises regarding rule compliance. Each exception weakens the rule and discredits the leader who tolerates it. The only certainty is that for a rule to play its regulatory role, it must be respected. In speaking of severity, what Sun Tzu asks for is rigor and consistency.

As the word severity disturbs some, I have chosen to replace it with "rigor," although I could have also spoken of "consistency" or even "firmness."

---

[7] https://www.EazyMirror.com/EPFS

In Practice

Once a rule tolerates exceptions, it becomes very difficult to determine where the limit of acceptability lies. To illustrate this challenge, let me share my experience: I led an executive training program where no absences were tolerated (Program A) and another program (Program B) where absences with good excuses did not require retaking the missed module.

In both cases, the rules were announced at the start.

Over the 15 years that Program A ran, some participants attempted to negotiate absences before realizing that no exceptions were tolerated. Once they understood that there was no hope for special treatment, everyone adapted to zero tolerance, and complaints ceased.

In Program B, there was not a single module where someone did not request an exception, with seemingly reasonable excuses. Each request required examination and decision making, but the boundary between acceptable and unacceptable reasons became increasingly blurred, making refusal more difficult.

Rigor in rule enforcement determines:

- The rules' effectiveness
- Time spent managing exceptions
- Simplification through zero tolerance (nothing to negotiate)
- Saves time and provides clarity

However, there is one essential condition: rules must be fair and legitimate. Strictly applying inappropriate rules would be self-defeating. Once the Engaged Team Charter, as described in Chap. 5, has been developed and adopted by the team, it should have the legitimacy required for rigorous application. This approach is certainly more legitimate than an old-style team charter or code of conduct imposed top–down.

The Engaged Team Charter significantly contributes to ensuring rule legitimacy. Speaking of "fair" rules means that they must be applied intelligently. This is where the sense of equity[8] comes into play, requiring discernment to:

- Treat specific situations uniquely when warranted
- Handle similar situations consistently
- Balance standardization with necessary flexibility

The combination of equity and rigor prevents potential excesses of strict enforcement. When equity guides the application of rules, it creates a framework

---

[8] Everything discussed about equity in Chap. 2 remains relevant to the sense of equity addressed here.

where rigor serves justice rather than becoming rigid or arbitrary. This balanced approach ensures that:

- Rules maintain their regulatory power
- Legitimate unique circumstances receive appropriate consideration
- Similar situations receive consistent treatment
- The spirit of the rule is honored alongside its letter

Lever 27 • Be Courageous

Among the most frequent criticisms of leaders, a lack of courage consistently ranks near the top. If employees so strongly expect courage from their leader, it suggests that this quality is rare in the professional world. A leader who lacks courage will never earn genuine respect or voluntary followership.

What is courage? Without venturing into philosophical reflection, two quotes sufficiently justify why a leader must be courageous:

- "Courage is the choice and willingness to confront agony, pain, danger, uncertainty, or intimidation."[9] When danger is faced without fear, it is rather called confidence or, more pejoratively, recklessness, especially when danger is underestimated.
- "Moral courage is the courage to take action for moral reasons despite the risk of adverse consequences,"[10] including in the face of popular opposition, shame, scandal, discouragement, or personal loss.

Courage requires fear, and genuine fear implies real danger. A leader incapable of placing themselves in dangerous situations to defend a cause just lacks courage. In essence, having courage means acting to defend a value while accepting the risk of losing something dear—whether it is social acceptance, bearing public criticism, or even financial loss.

The necessity for a leader to be courageous is so evident that justifying it risks stating the obvious. Skeptics need only look at the damage resulting from cowardice. Unfortunately, examples abound in the professional world.

---

[9] https://en.wikipedia.org/wiki/Courage

[10] https://en.wikipedia.org/wiki/Moral_courage

Once you have adopted an Engaged Team Charter,[11] you must have the courage to do whatever is required to enforce it. This is not easy, as you must face psychological pressures and various defensive tactics that people use, even when they are not justified.

The example of exemption requests and other exceptions is striking. If an employee wants to be absent or modify schedules for personal reasons, and you refuse based on fairness to others, it is very likely that the frustrated individual will be unhappy. They might:

- Display sullen behavior
- Turn others against you
- Rewrite the narrative to cast you as the villain
- Create coalitions of opposition

In such situations, you must choose between:

- Revealing your perspective to set the record straight
- Maintaining silence to protect the confidentiality of the frustrated individual's situation

To prevent such difficulties, it may be prudent to include in the Engaged Team Charter:

- A governance rule specifying that within the team, confidentiality may be lifted to justify or facilitate the application of fairness or caring
- Guiding principles for feedback to reduce the required courage and facilitate difficult conversations

The greatest courage is required for decisive action:

- Making decisions without excessive delay
- Avoiding unnecessary consultations or committee formations
- Accepting that decisions might not be perfect or popular
- Understanding that delayed decisions create domino effects throughout the organization

Courage also means:

- Accepting the possibility of mistakes or failure
- Embracing risk taking
- Overcoming various fears:
  - Fear of failure
  - Fear of displeasing superiors or colleagues
  - Fear of losing position
  - Fear of decreased popularity
  - Fear of changing successful past practices
  - Fear of going against the current

---

[11] See Chap. 5.

As noted above, fear is not the problem. The real issue lies in paralysis and the inability to overcome fear through action. This is precisely why courage is required.

A leader's credibility is essential for inspiring followers to willingly follow. This credibility will be:

- Dramatically affected by displays of cowardice
- Correspondingly enhanced by demonstrations of courage

You should engage in daily self-reflection by asking:
"What actions or decisions today have enhanced or reduced my team's perception of my courage?"
This simple yet powerful question serves multiple purposes:

- Maintains focus on courage as a daily practice
- Creates accountability for demonstrating brave leadership
- Helps to identify patterns of avoidance or bold action
- Reinforces the connection between courageous decisions and leadership credibility

Just as with trust, employees are best positioned to assess their leader's level of courage. The ultimate test, therefore, is straightforward: ask your team members anonymously about their perception of your courage level.
This assessment requires courage in itself, as it means:

- Facing potentially uncomfortable truths
- Opening oneself up to direct evaluation
- Accepting unfiltered feedback
- Confronting possible gaps between self-perception and reality

This test is naturally reserved for leaders who:

- Possess strong nerves
- Are prepared to face their reality, however sobering it might be
- Demonstrate the very courage they seek to measure
- Are committed to genuine self-improvement

Courage Pays Off
The tax administration decides to audit Grandfather and summons him to the tax office.

The tax inspector is not surprised when Grandfather shows up with his lawyer.

The auditor says, "Well sir, you have an extravagant lifestyle with no full-time employment, which you explain by saying you make money through betting. I must tell you that the tax office finds this hard to believe."

"I am a great gambler, and I can prove it," replies Grandfather. "I can even give you a demonstration."

The auditor thinks for a moment and says, "Alright. Go ahead!"
Grandfather responds, "I bet you 1000 euros that I can bite my eye."
The auditor thinks for a moment and says, "You're on!"
Grandfather removes his glass eye and bites it. The auditor's jaw drops.
Grandfather says, "Now, I bet 2000 euros that I can bite my other eye."
The auditor, knowing that Grandfather is not blind, accepts the bet.
Grandfather then removes his dentures and bites his good eye.
The stunned auditor now realizes he has bet and lost 3000 euros, with Grandfather's lawyer as witness. He starts getting very nervous.
"Would you like to go double or nothing?"
Grandfather responds, "I bet you 6000 euros that I can stand on one side of your desk and urinate into the wastepaper basket on the other side without a single drop falling in between."
The auditor, twice burned, is now very cautious but looks carefully and concludes that the old man could never pull this off. He agrees.
Grandfather stands beside the desk and opens his fly to proceed. Despite his efforts, he cannot make the stream reach the wastebasket on the other side. As a result, he soaks the auditor's entire desk.
The auditor is overjoyed, realizing that he has just turned a major defeat into a huge victory.
But Grandfather's lawyer groans and hits himself on the head with his right hand.
The confused auditor asks him, "What's wrong? Are you alright?"
"Not really," says the lawyer. "This morning, when Grandfather told me that he had been summoned for a tax audit, he bet me 25000 euros that he could come here, urinate on your desk, and you would actually be happy about it!"

Courage is intimately linked to resilience. Those who have sufficient self-confidence and faith in their ability to face adversity will be less paralyzed by fear and will find the inner resources to demonstrate courage.

Lever 28 • Ensure Congruence and Coherence

Humans are programmed for survival, which drives us to constantly monitor our environment for potential threats. The earlier we identify these threats, the more time we have to react appropriately. Those who can identify weak signals—early warning signs of threats or opportunities—before others gain a significant advantage. This identification ability requires careful attention to details, their evolution, and the coherence of what is observed. Each identified contradiction likely signals danger.

Because it is key to survival, humans are wired to monitor the coherence (logical consistency) of things—and people. Through this monitoring, people can determine whether their leader's behavior is authentic. As lack of authenticity signals unreliability, any inconsistency acts as a warning signal: when their leader claims to be attentive to people while checking messages during a colleague's presentation, they recognize the disconnect between words and actions. Based on this observation, they can no longer trust their statements or declarations.

Congruence (alignment between internal states and external behavior) expresses behavioral consistency through experience. In more practical terms, congruence means alignment between who you are (your core personality), what you think and feel (your convictions and values), and what you say or do.

You might perform actions that appear highly coherent but contradict your nonverbal communication. Consider the manager who tells their team that they have complete confidence in the new strategy and are receiving it calmly without stress, whereas their nervously tapping foot betrays them. Without alignment, their message fails to convince.

The challenge of being congruent lies in achieving perfect alignment on all levels. This is difficult in private life, but becomes more challenging in a professional context. In addition to the aforementioned alignments, it is also essential to align with your company's culture, strategy, and objectives. Each additional parameter increases complexity. How can you demonstrate humanity in a company exclusively focused on performance, where employees are seen merely as necessary resources that can be replaced by other "resources"? How can you avoid betraying your personal humanistic values while working for an anti-personnel mine manufacturer?

The second challenge lies in constant surveillance. You are not monitored by video cameras but by each employee. Unconsciously, and as part of their survival instinct, they attend to anything that might influence their environment to detect potential threats. As a leader, you are inherently a "climate maker" who primarily influences their environment, so they are programmed to carefully monitor your actions and gestures, particularly those beyond your conscious control.

The third challenge stems from the impossibility of completely controlling all communication channels. As with your nonverbal behavior or voice intonation, some channels are managed by your unconscious and will betray misalignment whether you want them to or not. As the saying goes, "You cannot hide your true colours." As you cannot maintain pretense sustainably and knowing that your nonverbal communication will eventually betray you, you have only two options: live in alignment or lose credibility.

The second option automatically reduces your employees' trust and engagement levels. How can you hope to inspire your employees to follow you if they doubt the congruence of what they observe? There is no way of bluffing…

In Practice

To achieve alignment across multiple parameters, you must:

- Know yourself well—which is far from a simple matter
- Demonstrate consistency in your thinking and actions

- Proactively employ common sense. Although this seems obvious, as one wit aptly observed, "If there is one thing that is not common, it is common sense."[12] Any deviation from common sense results in a loss of congruence

To maintain congruence in your daily leadership practice:

- Before making decisions, pause to check alignment with your stated values
- Regularly seek feedback from trusted colleagues about perceived inconsistencies
- Document your key principles and review your actions against them
- Practice mindfulness to stay aware of your nonverbal signals
- When facing difficult decisions, consider how you would explain your choice to your team
- Address inconsistencies promptly when they are pointed out
- Schedule regular reflection time to ensure that your actions align with your worldview

I emphasize common sense because your employees constantly use it as a benchmark to ensure that you think as they do (which is what they call common sense!). Common sense is, therefore, a highly relative concept. As explained earlier, not everyone uses the same filters to interpret reality.

The final word on congruence is that, like trust, it cannot be decreed. It depends on others' opinions and requires constant vigilance: each time you lack congruence, you lose points in your employees' engagement level. Philippe Rodet and Yves Desjacques emphatically add, "Inconsistency generates frustrations, tensions, and disengagement. It therefore promotes the emergence of negative emotions that translate into increased stress levels."[13]

Lever 29 • Demonstrate Wisdom/Discernment

Wisdom is the capacity for discernment—the ability to avoid falling victim to illusions or manipulations. It means exercising sound judgment to distinguish right from wrong (assuming that these notions represent shared concepts, as differing interpretations can lead to vastly different opinions from others) in accordance with the organization's imperatives.

To demonstrate discernment, you must first develop sufficient understanding of the situation. Wisdom requires clear-sightedness—an accurate and unbiased understanding of things. Each error in judgment, when analyzing received information, costs you credibility points... This presents an enormous challenge, as organizations contain many people who manipulate, filter, transform, and adapt information.

---

[12] This quote is commonly attributed to Mark Twain, though the original source is uncertain.

[13] Philippe Rodet and Yves Desjacques, "Le Management bienveillant," Eyrolles, 2017.

In Practice

To obtain unfiltered or unmanipulated information, you must identify reliable information sources among your employees. You also need to develop an extensive network of informants to access information from different sources.

Effective information gathering and verification require a systematic approach:

- Build a diverse network of trusted sources:
- Develop relationships across different departments
- Maintain connections at various organizational levels
- Cultivate informal channels of communication

  Verify information quality by:

- Cross-checking data from multiple sources
- Observing patterns and inconsistencies
- Maintaining regular contact with front-line employees
- Considering long-term implications beyond immediate benefits

  Practice discerning leadership by:

- Creating safe spaces for honest feedback
- Encouraging constructive dissent
- Demonstrating appreciation for truthful reporting, even when unfavorable
- Recognizing when seemingly positive news masks underlying problems
- Protecting information sources from potential retaliation

  Consider these practical examples:

- When a collaborator presents performance data, wisdom means:
  - Looking beyond surface numbers to understand context
  - Questioning unusual patterns without appearing accusatory
  - Considering both individual and systemic factors affecting results
- During conflict resolution, discernment requires:
  - Hearing all sides without preconceived or premature judgment
  - Identifying hidden agendas or unstated concerns
  - Distinguishing between symptoms and root causes

Criteria for Psychiatric Hospitalization
During a visit to a psychiatric hospital, I asked the director how he decided whether a patient should be institutionalized or not.

"Well," replied the director, "we fill a bathtub, then give the patient a teaspoon, a teacup, and a bucket, asking them to empty the bathtub."

"Oh, I understand," I said. "A normal person would use the bucket because it is bigger than the spoon or cup."

"No," replied the director. "A normal person would pull the plug. Would you like a bed near the window?"

4.4   Your Personality Traits for Caring Leadership

Lever 30 • Demonstrate Humanity

One widely cited definition of humanity is: "**Humanity signifies human love and compassion towards each other.**"[14] In other words, it is a disposition toward understanding and compassion for one's fellow humans, which leads to helping those in need. This aligns perfectly with caring. Someone who demonstrates humanity will naturally find it easier to behave in a caring manner.

An interesting question arises: to demonstrate humanity, must one wish well for everyone, or is it sufficient to wish well for a limited number of people? I am inclined to answer that the character trait of "humanity" should not be discriminatory. However, I can imagine that caring as a behavior might be limited to a specific group. Someone lacking the character trait of humanity might behave in a caring way only toward certain people. To illustrate this, I take an extreme case: a mafia leader would not hesitate to "eliminate" those perceived as adversaries or obstacles to their "business." Despite this manifest lack of humanity, it does not prevent them from being very caring toward clan members or being an attentive grandparent.

Even though one can occasionally demonstrate caring without humanity, it is much more difficult for someone who possesses humanity as a quality to lack caring.

In Chap. 2, caring was addressed as an imperative and an end in itself. The "caring" imperative differs from a behavior that benefits others, which is the specific and concrete manifestation of caring toward certain people in a given context. The character trait of "humanity" is an ingredient that significantly promotes beneficial behaviors. Just as activating fairness requires a sense of fairness as a character trait, I believe that activating caring requires a sense of humanity as a character trait.

I find it difficult to imagine that a manager could be sustainably caring toward their employees without a good measure of humanity. In this regard, humanity, as the fifth quality mentioned by Sun Tzu, appears as an essential component of Fair and Caring Leadership.

In Practice

As with all other character traits, it is difficult to realistically self-evaluate. The opinion of those around you is generally a better judge. Your employees' perception depends on the quality of communication established between them and you.

---

[14] https://en.wikipedia.org/wiki/Humanity_(virtue)

To measure your effectiveness, use anonymous feedback tools such as EazyMirror to ask staff to rate their perception of your level of caring. The anonymity of such quick surveys enables honest responses, providing valuable insights into how your caring leadership is perceived.

Finding the right balance in demonstrating humanity requires practical guidelines:

- Demonstrate caring through consistent small actions rather than grand gestures
- Acknowledge individual circumstances without compromising professional boundaries
- Share the reasoning behind caring decisions to help others to understand your motivations
- Document caring initiatives and their positive impacts without self-promotion
- Create opportunities for team members to share their experiences of receiving support
- Make caring visible through systematic practices rather than occasional displays

For a detailed analysis of the psychological levers of malevolence and caring, I recommend Paul-Marie Chavanne and Olivier Truong's book.[15] Beyond examining the feasibility of caring in business, they describe the connection between people's psychological profiles and their capacity for demonstrating caring. They confirm that caring is not within everyone's reach.

Faced with this reality and knowing that the absence of caring is contagious, my conclusion is that, unless you are masochistic, you should never surround yourself with people incapable of caring. I simply avoid them.

Lever 31 • Develop Your Emotional Intelligence

Emotional intelligence is commonly defined as the ability to recognize, understand, and manage one's own emotions as well as recognize, understand, and deal with others' emotions. Given the wealth of literature highlighting the importance and impact of this competency on success, professional and personal satisfaction, relationship quality, and other related aspects, there is no need to repeat what many others have already said. I will focus on several points that seem important in the context of Fair and Caring Leadership.

In Practice

To act in your employees' best interests, you must first understand not only what those interests are but also their emotions. Without this understanding, you might take actions that serve someone's interests but do so awkwardly, given their current emotional state.

---

[15] Olivier Truong and Paul-Marie Chavanne, op. cit.

Consider this example, which many couples will recognize: one partner has experienced a difficult situation and recounts it in great detail to their significant other. The latter, wanting to help their loved one, offers suggestions on how to handle the situation. These suggestions are poorly received because the person sharing was not looking for solutions—they just needed to vent. In the end, both parties feel frustrated because neither decoded the other's emotional state.

To better read emotional states, practice these techniques:

- Pay attention to non-verbal cues: body language, tone of voice, and facial expressions often reveal more than words
- Listen actively without planning your response—focus on understanding rather than solving
- Notice changes in someone's usual behavior patterns or communication style
- Create safe spaces for authentic expression by demonstrating empathy and withholding judgment
- Ask open-ended questions to better understand emotional context
- Validate emotions before moving to solutions or actions
- Check your understanding by reflecting back on what you have heard and observed

Good intentions are not enough—others must understand things the same way you do. As their ability to understand is inevitably influenced by their emotional state, you must be receptive to and capable of decoding it. Without this ability, you risk making missteps that ultimately achieve the opposite of your intended result. This demonstrates that emotional intelligence requires dual competency:

- First toward yourself
- Then toward others

Having only one of these is insufficient.

Fair process, as described later, heavily depends on emotional intelligence. Identifying the right moment and the right way to say something requires considerable emotional intelligence. I remember once having to make a decision about terminating an employee just before Christmas. To avoid ruining his holiday and celebrations, I thought it might be better to announce it upon their return. On the other hand, he might have resented learning about it afterward because, had he known earlier, he could have spent less during the holidays. This example shows that:

- Being caring alone is not enough for others to perceive it
- There are no one-size-fits-all solutions
- You must inevitably adapt to people, circumstances, and their emotional states

In Practice

A complementary challenge is anticipating the emotions that you may trigger through your actions or communications. This complexity affects not only the person directly concerned but also all other employees who witness the situation. Although they may not be directly impacted, they observe and draw conclusions from what you say or do. Their reactions depend on their emotional state and their perception of fairness and caring.

Your emotional intelligence is challenged on multiple levels:

- Managing the emotions of the directly affected person
- Handling the emotional responses of observers
- Anticipating ripple effects throughout the organization
- Building and maintaining trust during difficult situations

Trust capital plays a crucial role in emotional management. Everything you say or do will be interpreted based on the level of trust your team members have in you. A high level of trust creates more forgiveness and the benefit of the doubt. A low level of trust leads people to use observations to reinforce previous negative opinions.

As one observer wisely noted: "People will forget what you said, people will forget what you did, but people will never forget how you made them feel."[16] Although logical minds may focus on content, what really impacts others and their trust level is their emotional experience, regardless of whether it seems justified or rational.

The good news about emotional intelligence is that unlike the Intelligent Quotient (IQ), emotional intelligence can be significantly improved through dedicated effort. Research shows that emotional intelligence training—outperforming control groups and even theatrical improvisation training[17]—improves:

- Physical and mental health
- Overall satisfaction
- Relationships
- Employability

For those seeking concrete validation, emotional intelligence can be measured through Emotional Quotient (EQ) assessments, similar to IQ tests.[18]

Remember   Those who can understand and manage their own emotions while positively influencing others' emotions are best positioned to become excellent leaders.

---

[16] Commonly attributed to Maya Angelou, although the original source is uncertain.

[17] Moïra Mikolajczak, Catholic University of Louvain, Sciences et Avenir, December 2010.

[18] The University of Geneva has developed a test that appears to be a reference standard for measuring the EQ: http://nantys.ch/product/emco4/?lang=en

The Importance of Emotion Management
A husband's text to his wife, "Honey, a car hit me while leaving my office. Jacqueline brought me to the hospital. Right now, doctors are running tests and taking X-rays. Severe head injuries, but no risk of lasting effects. The wound required nineteen stitches. I also have three broken ribs, a broken arm, and a major fracture in my left leg. They're considering amputating my right foot. I love you."

The wife's response: "Who is Jacqueline?"

Lever 32 • Be Humble and Vulnerable

Humility naturally leads to showing consideration for others. "The antidote to arrogance is expressing humility,"[19] which reinforces the value of capitalizing on employees' strengths. The opposites of humility—arrogance and contempt—manifest as haughty, hurtful behavior that is clearly incompatible with caring leadership.

As I have never met anyone who enjoys being treated in a haughty and hurtful manner, I have always wondered why some people continue to display arrogance or its corollary, contempt. Not seeing the benefit that they gain from being disliked by others, and knowing that behaviors are never without purpose, I have concluded that their behavior is not dictated by its impact on others but on themselves. Their likely unconscious goal being perhaps to assert themselves or seek reassurance, their arrogance seems merely an expression of a lack of self-confidence.

Another hypothesis remains: the arrogant person sincerely believes that people are fooled and appreciate being hurt or treated haughtily. If this is the case, they display stupidity and would benefit from measuring their EQ to open their eyes.

Whatever justifies arrogance, one certainty remains: as it does not inspire trust, there is only one solution—prohibit it.

Its antithesis, humility, is a necessity. It expresses acceptance of one's limits and weaknesses. As no one is perfect, those who pretend to be are destined to stumble sooner or later. Because one person's perfection accentuates others' weaknesses, employees rarely forgive a leader's supposed perfection, as it makes them feel diminished.

I sense that employees always compare themselves with their leader:

- First to determine if they have the characteristics required to take their place someday
- Then to verify that they understand them

Alignment with the leader allows them to feel secure, particularly by displaying behaviors that please them. This is an indirect component of the survival instinct mentioned earlier.

---

[19] Philippe Rodet and Yves Desjacques, "Le Management bienveillant," Eyrolles, 2017.

In Practice

Acknowledging one's limitations demonstrates humility and humanity. By preventing your employees from feeling inferior to a "perfect" leader, you contribute to their self-esteem. The "perfect" leader, by definition caring, should therefore do everything possible to improve their employees' self-confidence. The paradox of the perfect leader is that they must reveal their imperfections; if they appear flawless, they risk making their employees feel inadequate. Therefore, the truly "perfect" leader must demonstrate that they are not perfect.

Examples of appropriate vulnerability in leadership include:

- Openly acknowledging when you do not have all the answers and seeking input from your team
- Sharing past professional mistakes and what you learned from them
- Admitting when you need help understanding complex technical aspects of your team's work
- Taking responsibility for decisions that did not yield expected results
- Being transparent about challenges you are working to overcome
- Asking for feedback on your leadership style and implementing changes
- Sharing moments of doubt or uncertainty about some decisions while maintaining a clear direction

Your humility also demonstrates that you are vulnerable, like everyone else. By acknowledging your mistakes, you implicitly give your employees permission to make some as well (I refer to legitimate mistakes made in good faith, not those from negligence or laziness). This permission makes them feel secure, reducing the pressure and stress that they would experience if they had to strive for perfection.

Unlike the superhero image of always doing everything right, employees respect and appreciate a leader who acknowledges their vulnerability. This expresses the fact that you cannot do everything alone and need your employees' support and assistance. When you falter, they will help you to find solutions or overcome the difficulty encountered. However, if you have been arrogant, then stumble, they will push your head underwater. Showing humility increases your own resilience and that of your team.

The Virtues of Humility

A young boy enters a barbershop, and the barber whispers to his client, "This is the most stupid child in the world. Watch what happens."

The barber takes a one-euro coin in one hand and a fifty-cent coin in the other, then calls the boy and asks, "Which one would you prefer, son?"

The boy takes the fifty-cent coin and leaves the one-euro coin.

"What did I tell you?" whispers the barber. "This kid never learns!"

Later, while leaving, the client sees the same young boy coming out of a grocery store with a chocolate ice cream and says, "Hey, son! May I ask you a question? Why did you take the fifty-cent coin instead of the one-euro coin?"

The boy licks his ice cream and responds: "Because the day I take the one-euro coin, the game will be over!"

Lever 33 • Know Yourself without Self-Deception

It is essential to know yourself well to understand not only how to make the best use of your strengths but also how to compensate for your weaknesses. This self-knowledge requires considerable clarity and humility.[20] By knowing where you might need help, you can rely on your employees' strengths.

Asking for help or advice is not a sign of weakness, but rather an acknowledgment of others' competence. They will be grateful to you for this recognition. You do not need to diminish yourself but acknowledge that your employees also possess skills that you do not. This is the expression of team strength.

In Practice

To know yourself well, various methods are available. In addition to the previously mentioned strengths-based leadership approach, there are numerous profiling tests such as MBTI, HBDI, L.A.B.E.L., Leonardo, and their counterparts. The existence of multiple tests expresses a simple reality: none of them is complete or exhaustive. The fact that all these tests coexist indicates that each has advantages that appeal to certain experts, but also that none of them is sufficiently superior to render the others irrelevant. We can reasonably conclude that they overlap and complement each other, but none alone is sufficient. Even if we were to use them all cumulatively, I am not even certain that they could provide a complete picture of human complexity. When using them, it is essential to keep their limitations in mind, without falling into the trap of unconditional faith in a single test.

You can also engage a coach or assessment specialists. Or conduct a "360°" evaluation, though you must be aware that, like all profiling tests, each 360° is aimed at highlighting certain characteristics without providing an exhaustive view. The ideal would be to use a tool such as www.EazyMirror.com that allows you to personalize questions to get answers to what interests YOU.

There is another, often underutilized, method that complements your own observation capacity: asking your employees, peers, and leaders to share their perceptions of you. If you have established and maintained a relationship of trust,

---

[20] "He who is aware of his limitations is closest to perfection"—Goethe.

they should not hesitate to tell you the truth. This presupposes that you have implemented a feedback culture.[21] Knowing how you are perceived is an invaluable gift and often closer to reality than the potentially biased image that you might have of yourself.

Finally, beware of falling into the trap of personal blindness, which involves remaining locked in your beliefs without being attentive to subtle signals from those around you. Those who never feel responsible and blame others are very often victims of personal blindness. It is akin to the poor teacher who blames students for not listening or lacking motivation to learn while delivering a deadly boring lecture. Knowing yourself well requires a large dose of clarity, humility, and the ability to question yourself and acknowledge your mistakes. Here again, this is not within everyone's reach…

To overcome personal blindness, consider these practical strategies:

- Actively seek contradictory views:
  - Regularly ask "What am I missing?"
  - Encourage team members to challenge your assumptions
  - Create safe spaces for honest and constructive disagreement
- Implement structured reflection practices:
  - Keep a leadership journal documenting decisions and their outcomes
  - Schedule regular self-assessment sessions
  - Review past situations where your initial perception proved incorrect
- Develop specific counter-habits:
  - When blaming others, ask "What was my role in this?"
  - Before defending your position, articulate the opposing viewpoint
  - Practice saying, "I might be wrong about this"
- Create feedback mechanisms:
  - Use anonymous suggestion systems
  - Schedule regular "perception checks" with diverse team members
  - Establish mentor relationships with experienced leaders
- Watch for warning signs of personal blindness:
  - Consistently believing you are right whereas others are wrong
  - Dismissing feedback as irrelevant or incorrect
  - Finding yourself surprised by others' reactions to your decisions
  - Noticing that people have stopped offering alternative viewpoints

Remember: Overcoming personal blindness is an ongoing process, not a one-time achievement. The goal is not to eliminate blind spots entirely (which is impossible) but to develop systems for identifying and addressing them more effectively.

---

[21] See Lever 50 in Chap. 5.

Lever 34 • No Cowardice

The necessity of demonstrating courage having already been established, some might be tempted to think that the absence of courage equals cowardice. However, this is not the case. Given the toxicity of cowardice, it is important to emphasize that the rejection of cowardice is a valuable quality in its own right.

Lacking courage is not as unhealthy as displaying cowardice:

- Lacking courage means not daring to act
- Cowardice means causing harm

  For example:

- Lacking courage may mean accepting team downsizing without daring to challenge those who made the decision
- Cowardice would mean terminating the most vulnerable employees because their capacity to retaliate is lesser

A manager who lacks courage will not be a source of inspiration, whereas one who is cowardly will be a source of contempt. Cowardice is such an abhorred flaw that the manager who displays it destroys all chances of being followed. The cowardly leader can never have engaged employees. Thus, they can never be a leader.

Lever 35 • Find Sources of Gratification and Joy in Interaction and Leadership

Good leaders find significant sources of gratification in interacting with their employees and in leading. Not only do their teams express their appreciation in various ways, but performance is optimal. The leader is thus doubly rewarded.

In line with the proverb, "You cannot pour from an empty cup," you must first eliminate your own discomfort and find joy in leading. Pleasure is just as contagious for your teams as passion. If your employees do not find pleasure in coming to work, their level of engagement will suffer. And for them to find pleasure, you must experience it yourself. The absence of genuine pleasure is always noticed by team members, because in management, you simply cannot fake it.

The best way to make pleasure last is to have some. As with everything, it is not possible to have only pleasure. In every activity, some tasks are less rewarding than others, but overall, moments of gratification must outweigh the less pleasant ones. This is obviously also true for leadership.

If the overall balance is not positive, something is wrong. You have two options: correct your approach (this book is aimed at helping you to improve your leadership) or accept that being a leader might not suit you.

Remaining in a leadership role solely for the compensation, status, or title—without genuine enjoyment—is ultimately detrimental to both the leader and their team.

I strongly advise against this path as you will likely pay for it with deteriorating health. Your circle will also pay through frustration or even health issues.

If you do not find pleasure in leadership:

- Your employees will feel less engaged
- They will assign you a lower engagement score than if pleasure were present

The only problem is that pleasure cannot be forced. You either have it because you are doing what you love, or you do not have it at all. **There must be an alignment between your interactions with employees and your basic personality.** Without this, there can be no pleasure and no well-being for either you or your teams.

In Practice

Specific ways to cultivate genuine enjoyment in leadership include:

- Focus on growth moments:
  - Celebrate team members' development milestones
  - Take pride in watching employees master new skills
  - Document progress to remind yourself of positive changes
- Create meaningful connections:
  - Schedule regular informal check-ins beyond task discussions
  - Show genuine interest in team members' professional aspirations
  - Share appropriate personal insights to build authentic relationships
- Design enjoyable leadership practices:
  - Transform routine meetings into engaging discussions
  - Incorporate elements of play into problem-solving sessions
  - Create traditions that the team looks forward to
- Cultivate personal satisfaction:
  - Identify aspects of leadership that naturally energize you
  - Delegate tasks that drain your enthusiasm to people who enjoy them
  - Develop your own leadership style rather than imitating others
- Build positive feedback loops:
  - Notice and acknowledge when interactions feel genuinely pleasurable
  - Reflect on successful leadership moments
  - Share your enjoyment openly when appropriate

You can use the above checklist as an initial indicator to gauge how much you enjoy leading and interacting with your team members.

Lever 36 • Act in a Caring Way

This lever was already addressed in Chap. 2 within the framework of the reflection on caring leadership.

4.5   Visual Summary: Fair and Caring Leadership Traits

Figure 4.1 provides a visual summary of the Fair and Caring Leadership levers associated with leader personality traits.

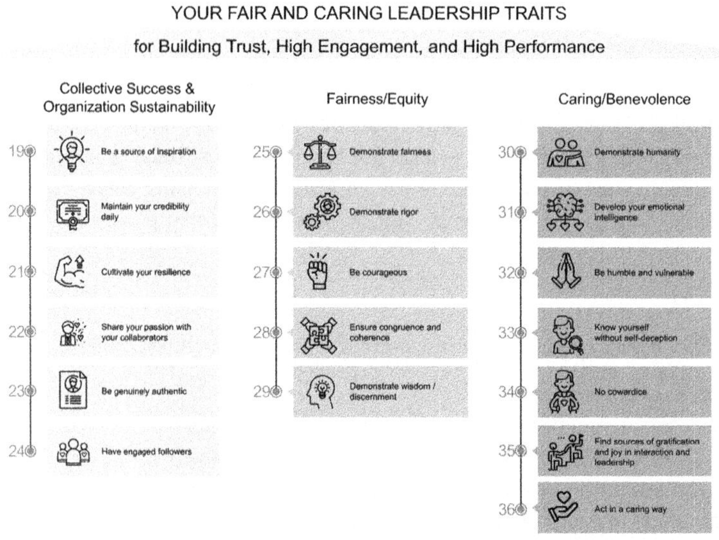

Fig. 4.1 Summary of Fair and Caring Leadership levers connected to leader personality traits

Establish an Operating Framework That Fosters Engagement

5

5.1   The Team Governance Model for Collective Success

To build trust, applying all the previous principles is not enough. It is also necessary to establish framework conditions that make your employees feel secure by clarifying the rules of the game. These can exist both at the organization level (i.e., those mentioned in Chap. 2) and/or at the team level.

This chapter presents a proven team governance model. Managers who have used it have improved:

- Their quality of life
- Their team members' engagement levels
- Their team's overall performance

Because it suits some managers but not others, it is up to you to evaluate how you can benefit from it, considering your worldview.

The proposed governance mechanism at the team level is based on a specific team charter. This charter is called the "Engaged Team Charter." It consists of six pillars that form a complete whole. I also call this "the six-stage rocket" (see Fig. 5.1). Each pillar serves as a lever. These levers are explained further below.

To help you understand the architecture of the Engaged Team Charter, I have grouped the six levers that compose it, setting aside the numerical order of the summary table. I hope that you will forgive me for twisting this sequence.

Co-creating and then living by an Engaged Team Charter has a proven positive impact on most teams that trust their leader: it boosts trust within the team and toward its leader.

"Introduction and Warnings" for this book are available in Front matter and "Epilogue" and "Complete Framework for Building Trust, High Engagement, and High Performance" are available in Back matter. Readers can download them free from https://doi.org/10.1007/978-3-032-05172-1.

R. H Cohen, *Driving Employee Engagement*, Management for Professionals, https://doi.org/10.1007/978-3-032-05172-1_5

37	Meaningful purpose	• Gives meaning • Gives direction towards the purpose
38	Indicators of success	• Clarify the purpose • Make the purpose tangible / implementable
43	Imperatives	• Clarify what everyone is entitled to expect and what can be enforced • Framework for decision-making
54	Expected behaviors	• Clarify people interaction • Provide a point of reference for periodic evaluations
44	Governance rules	• Clarify the rules of the game • Make the culture explicit
45	Protection measures	• Protect those who comply with the Team Charter • Make everyone feel safe

Fig. 5.1 The six-stage rocket (Engaged Team Charter) for working harmoniously together

This team-level charter complements existing organization-wide fundamental principles (values, imperatives, non-negotiables, ten commandments, etc.). Each team must ensure that its governance is compatible with the organization's overall fundamental or non-negotiable principles.

Implementation requires one prerequisite: team members must have enough trust in their leader. If you have lost that trust, restoring it to support open discussion of the Engaged Team Charter will be challenging. A coach or facilitator might help, but there is no guarantee of success.

Lever 37 • Agree on a Meaningful Purpose for the Team

The first pillar involves formulating the unit's purpose to clarify the ultimate goal that must be collectively achieved. When discussing this with managers whom I train, I frequently notice confusion between the "what" and the "what for." While people generally understand the "what" that describes their activities (the mission), the purpose (the "what for") is often much less well understood.

To illustrate this, consider the example of companies with a training center. What is its purpose? Training-center employees have suggested various possibilities, including:

• Preparing a quality training catalog enabling everyone to acquire needed skills
• Promoting a learning culture
• Providing employees with optimal training opportunities at minimal cost to the company
• Supporting line operations by teaching necessary skills
• Developing competencies

- Encouraging employees to acquire skills and support their personal development
- Improving employee employability (which differs from "giving employees the means of improving their employability")

This demonstrates that for the same organizational function (training), there are very different perspectives on purpose. The purpose ultimately chosen by the team directly influences all members' behavior. Moreover, it has an enormous impact on how all employees interacting with the training center experience it. The reception and treatment given to internal clients will vary significantly depending on these different purposes.

The major challenge arises when I ask team members individually to share their understanding of their team's purpose. To date, I have never encountered a situation where every team member articulates the same purpose. This indicates that, unconsciously, each person makes daily operational choices based on their perception of the team's purpose. When team members do not share a common understanding, this misalignment means that everyone is not pulling in the same direction.

In Practice

Having your team debate its purpose will lead to an aligned understanding among all members. This discussion allows each person to internalize the purpose and integrate it into their work.

A collectively agreed-upon purpose has the merit of being the team's creation ("their baby") rather than simply yours, which would only engage you personally. A purpose co-constructed by the team engages each of its members.

Be careful, however, to avoid falling into the trap of adopting meaningless or generic purposes, or those designed primarily to glorify the leader's achievements. This often occurs when participants seek to "be recognized" as the best, smartest leaders, the most skilled, or as the leading authority in their field. These serve personal ego rather than true purpose. To gain clarity and perspective, it can be helpful to consult with a qualified expert when developing an appropriate purpose.

Beyond motivating teams, an explicit purpose can facilitate conflict management. It becomes highly valuable to determine whether contested behavior is aimed at serving the team's purpose or merely individual interests. When purpose remains unclear, the resulting ambiguity allows some to justify behaviors that may become sources of conflict.

A clear purpose serves as:

- A decision-making compass for evaluating actions and behaviors
- An objective reference point during disagreements
- A tool for distinguishing between purpose-driven and self-serving choices
- A framework for resolving conflicts based on shared understanding
- A shield against individual agendas that might disrupt team harmony

Lever 38 • Agree on Success Indicators for the Team's Purpose

Once the purpose is explicit, your team must choose indicators to verify how well this purpose is being realized. They will in practice measure the team's performance level. What is the value of setting a purpose if you never know how well you are achieving it?

Indicators make the purpose tangible and easy to understand at the operational level. Their value lies in helping all unit members to effectively understand and internalize the collective, concrete purpose. This is especially true when indicators are defined collectively. As they define what will be measured, Key Indicators of Success (KISs) drive people to take actions that influence what is measured.

As what is measured influences behavior automatically, KISs are a powerful means of mobilizing the team to realize the purpose. When everyone has thoroughly internalized the measurable goal, this alignment facilitates the leader's work considerably.

Two distinct categories of indicators must be distinguished:

- KISs: measure ends in themselves and verify purpose realization
- KPIs: measure the means or processes implemented to improve KISs

Taking the example of a training center whose purpose is to improve employee employability and operational effectiveness, let us examine why certain measures are KPIs rather than KISs:

Traditional KPIs that do not measure purpose achievement:

- Employee satisfaction with training: being satisfied does not necessarily mean improved employability or operational effectiveness
- Number of course participants: having many attendees is not the ultimate goal but rather a way of verifying if training resources are reaching enough people
- Course-quality evaluations: a course might be well-received without contributing to employability or operational effectiveness

Although common in training centers, these three indicators are inadequate for measuring purpose achievement, as none captures the ultimate goal of improving employees' employability and operational effectiveness.

For the training center that I counseled, we developed four purpose-aligned KISs, which were adopted after rich discussion and minor adjustments:

- Employee perception of how the training center contributes to their employability
- Employee perception of how the training center improves their operational effectiveness
- Leaders' perception of how the training center improves their teams' operational effectiveness
- Composite index of the training center's staff pride + engagement + satisfaction with fairness and caring

Important note about precision: Indicators do not need to be exact to be useful. Like a fuel gauge that gives approximate but sufficient information, KISs can be approximate while remaining a valuable tool for guidance and improvement.

In Practice

Just as with purpose, it is imperative that KISs are chosen by team members themselves.[1] When an indicator is selected by the team to measure its success, its use becomes meaningful. It gains legitimacy, unlike indicators imposed top–down. The latter are perceived as control tools, whereas team-chosen KISs are seen as a means of measuring the team members' ability to achieve what they desire.

The KISs serve as an extraordinary recognition tool by demonstrating measurably how well the team has delivered on its purpose. They measure both:

- Progress already achieved
- Distance remaining to reach the ambition

As recognition is a primary component of fairness, this building block is essential in the structure aimed at maintaining trust.

Lever 43 • Agree on Team Imperatives

The third pillar of the Engaged Team Charter involves collectively agreeing on the imperatives[2] (see Chap. 2) that must govern team operations and member interactions. As noted further on, these imperatives complement organization-wide non-negotiable fundamental principles at the team level. These non-negotiable imperatives at the team level must:

- Not only create obligations but also provide rights
- Be freely adopted by the team

Team imperatives differ from the organization's fundamental principles in several key ways:

- Scope: team imperatives address specific team dynamics and operations, whereas the organization's fundamental principles cover broader company-wide rights and obligations

---

[1] These KISs are not incompatible with KPIs that might have been defined by other parts of the organization, for example, as part of a balanced scorecard. Each entity defines what is important from its own perspective.

[2] As the six levers of the Engaged Team Charter are spread across three imperatives of the Complete Framework for Building Trust, High Engagement, and High Performance, the book addresses them in narrative order rather than numerical sequence. Each lever is numbered to help you connect it back to the framework as you go.

- Specificity: team imperatives can be more detailed and contextual to team needs and activity
- Implementation: team imperatives can be adjusted more readily to team circumstances
- Ownership: team imperatives are collectively developed and owned by team members
- Monitoring: team imperatives can be observed and reinforced through daily interactions

Examples of Potential Team Imperatives

- Collective interest takes precedence over individual interest
- No one receives special privileges
- No retaliation against those who speak the truth or report problematic situations
- Issues must be addressed within seven working days of occurrence—after this window, they cannot be raised
- Team members actively support other team members during high-workload periods (solidarity)
- We ensure that all team members have a voice in key decisions
- We maintain work–life boundaries for sustainable performance

---

In Practice

Team imperatives are essential for guiding decisions and actions that the rest of the Engaged Team Charter might not specify. They serve as the guiding thread that brings focus back to what is essential and help address ambiguous situations by providing a clear reference point.

Below are several illustrations of how the above team imperatives can help. Conflict Resolution:

Situation: team member raises issue from two months ago

Relevant Imperative: "Issues must be addressed within seven working days of occurrence"

Guidance: focus on current and future solutions rather than revisiting past issues

Resource Allocation:

Situation: one team member consistently gets challenging projects

Relevant Imperative: "We rotate challenging assignments to build collective capability"

Guidance: redistribute assignments to ensure balanced development opportunities

Work Overload:

Situation: team member working late regularly to meet deadlines

Relevant Imperatives:

"We maintain work–life boundaries for sustainable performance"
"We actively support team members during high-workload periods"

Guidance: redistribute work and provide additional support rather than accepting overtime as normal

Lever 54 • Specify Expected Behaviors within the Team

The fourth pillar of the Engaged Team Charter contains the catalog of behaviors expected from team members toward their colleagues and their leader, and vice versa. These behaviors are freely chosen by team members, in contrast to behavioral directives imposed top–down by their leader.

To illustrate potential themes for this pillar, consider these questions:

- Is it acceptable to receive and send messages during meetings?
- Is it acceptable to arrive late to a meeting?
- Is it acceptable to work remotely?
- Is it acceptable to criticize absent colleagues?
- Is it acceptable to take initiatives?
- Is it acceptable to never express recognition for work accomplished?
- Is it acceptable to not be accountable?
- Is it acceptable to express frustrations?

This exercise might seem patronizing and unnecessary, especially to those who are under the illusion that others think like they do and share their expectations. Most people fall into the trap of silent suppositions.[3] Each person has their own perspective on each subject. Sometimes, a perspective is shared with others on one topic, but it is unlikely to be the case across all topics.

Experience demonstrates the complexity of behavioral expectations. In one implementation of an Engaged Team Charter at Nestlé, the team identified more than 130 expected behaviors—a number that the team initially thought was too high. When it was suggested that superfluous ones should be removed, animated discussion led not only to the removal of a handful of behaviors but also to the identification of additional needed behaviors, resulting in roughly the same total. I have seen the same scenario repeatedly in the Engaged Team Charter workshops I have facilitated: teams consistently discover that the number of expected behaviors exceeds their initial expectations.

This reveals that what seems obvious to some is far from obvious to others when explicitly discussing group relationships. The underlying idea of this system rests on a collective agreement for expected behaviors, whatever they may be.

---

[3] Christian Morel, "*Les Décisions absurdes*," Gallimard, 2012.

Expected behaviors can include requirements for the leader. Employees can explicitly state what they expect from you. Although Chap. 3 presents behaviors that I recommend for being a fair and caring leader, you and your team might choose others.

The Engaged Team Charter should serve as a reference during periodic reviews (annual, evaluation, development, etc.), facilitating comparison between each person's actual behaviors/attitudes and those explicitly documented in the charter.

This illustrates the crucial difference between implicit and explicit expectations. Although anyone can claim to have misunderstood an implicit expectation, this becomes much harder to claim for behaviors that were not only written down but collectively chosen by the group.

Explicit expected behaviors create clarity and prevent conflicts:

- Everyone understands what they are expected to do and what is not acceptable
- Reduced ambiguity leads to fewer interpretations and conflicts

The preventive effect is strengthened because behaviors were defined by all team members rather than imposed by the leader.

When conflicts do arise (which can never be avoided entirely), the Engaged Team Charter provides:

- A reference point to identify which expected behavior was not respected and by whom
- Legitimacy for decisions or recommendations related to the conflict
- A framework that makes resolutions more acceptable and therefore more equitable

Lever 44 • Agree on Team Governance Rules

The fifth stage of the rocket includes governance rules that establish principles to be respected within the team. To illustrate the types of questions these rules can address, here are some examples (although this list, of course, is not exhaustive):

- The right to make mistakes and fail (in good faith, obviously)
  - Challenging assignments are rotated to build collective capabilities
- The way people are promoted, such as:
  - Time-based promotion (based on seniority)
  - Performance-based promotion (as a reward)
  - Competency-based promotion (when an employee has the most skills required for increased responsibilities)
- Project selection must be based on published and transparent criteria (such as those mentioned in lever 41 below)

These governance rules complement the imperatives and expected behaviors to define the culture that the team wishes to develop internally.

Note on classification: The distinction between an imperative and a governance rule is not always clear-cut. Although this distinction has theoretical merit, in practice, the classification matters less than ensuring that the principle is explicitly stated in the team charter. Whether a rule appears in the imperatives section or the governance rules section is less important than its clear documentation and teamwide understanding.

Lever 45 • Agree on Protective Measures with an Internal Justice System

The sixth stage of the rocket sets out the indispensable mechanisms for enforcing the Engaged Team Charter. A charter only makes sense if it is lived and respected.

Those who follow rules are always at a disadvantage compared with those who break them without consequences. For example:

- If there is no parking enforcement, searching for a legal spot is more constraining than parking in prohibited areas (which is very tempting when you know that nobody enforces the rule!)
- In examinations, honest students are disadvantaged compared with uncaught cheaters

---

In Practice

Protection of rule-followers is essential to maintain fairness and prevent them from becoming victims of those who transgress the rules. Those who respect the Engaged Team Charter must be protected through specific measures—the fundamental purpose of the rocket's sixth stage.

Failing to protect the team would be both unfair and uncaring toward its members who respect the rules. Consider these key points:

- Not implementing protective measures demonstrates a lack of fairness
- Absence of consequences for transgressions indirectly encourages charter violations
- Without protection, the entire system is likely to fail

Practical Protection Measures:

- Agreed-upon consequences for charter violations
- Transparent reporting mechanisms
- Confidential channels for raising concerns
- Swift and fair handling of reported issues
- Regular review of protection effectiveness
- Equal application of consequences regardless of position

Remember: The absence of protection mechanisms does not create a neutral situation—it actively disadvantages those who follow the rules while rewarding those who do not.

Although this sixth stage could technically be part of the governance rules of the fifth stage, years of experience have shown that this matter is so crucial that it deserves its own "stage" in the rocket. This separate treatment ensures that team members give it the attention that it deserves. When protection measures are merely included within governance rules, people often find creative ways to avoid addressing this uncomfortable topic. Making it a separate stage makes it harder to sidestep this essential aspect.

In Practice

EazyMirror (www.EazyMirror.com) offers the following effective three-phase system to foster the enforcement of Engaged Team Charters:

Phase 1—Team-Level Assessment:

- Team selects charter components to evaluate
- Anonymous questionnaire measures compliance level (scale 0–4)
- Each member expresses their perception of how well the team lives each component
- Results identify problem areas

Phase 2—Individual Anonymous Feedback:

- For components of phase 1 with unsatisfactory scores, members evaluate each other's level of compliance (custom mutual 360)
- EazyMirror consolidates feedback while maintaining anonymity
- Each member receives their consolidated scores only
- This creates personal awareness without public judgment or finger-pointing
- Individuals can identify needed behavioral changes to improve their scores

Phase 3—Optional Score Sharing:

- After agreed-upon measurement iterations, members may choose to share the latest scores teamwide
- Only those who did not take advantage of the time they had before disclosure to improve their scores become accountable
- Prospect of transparency motivates behavioral improvement
- This deferred disclosure avoids immediate discomfort of sharing insufficient scores

This progressive approach:

- Maintains psychological safety
- Provides clear metrics
- Encourages self-improvement
- Builds toward accountability
- Preserves anonymity when needed
- Supports behavioral change without judgment until disclosure

Once rules are defined in an Engaged Team Charter, it is necessary to establish:

- Mechanisms for resolving differences in interpretation
- Conflict-resolution procedures
- Decision-making processes including:
  - Who has the authority to make judgments (judges or arbitrators)
  - How decisions are made (individually, by the majority, unanimously)
  - Available appeal processes

Although an internal justice system need not be as complex as civil justice, each group needs one that provides security for its members. Without such a system, unchecked power can lead to arbitrary decisions or even dictatorship, leaving team members without recourse.

In Practice

As a fair and caring leader, you should aspire to more than being perceived as a dictator. It is your responsibility to establish an internal justice system that provides security for your team.

Your internal justice system should define:

- Nonretroactivity of rules
- Appeal procedures
- Number of arbitrators or judges required
- Decision-making processes
- Fundamental principles to be respected

The format for this internal justice system can be flexible:

- A simple code of ethics defining core principles
- A more detailed document outlining specific procedures
- A combination of basic principles with supplementary guidelines

This particular charter structure is called an "Engaged Team Charter" because it results in member engagement, largely due to its collective definition and adoption by the team, supported by an internal justice mechanism.

Lever 42 • Align the Engaged Team Charter with Fundamental Principles of the Organization

To maintain behavioral consistency within an organization, leadership, the board of directors, and/or shareholders should establish fundamental principles. These are the core values and principles that everyone must respect within the organization. They serve as the organization's constitution or, like the Ten

Commandments' societal aspects (without religious connotations), provide essential guidelines. Because fundamental principles are non-negotiable, every member of the organization must adhere to these principles, regardless of their position. Ideally, an independent internal justice system should also enforce them.

The fundamental principles may include elements derived from organizational values or imperatives. An example of a fundamental principle could be "Treat employees and business partners fairly." Suppose the three imperatives suggested in the PFC model from Chap. 2 are included. In that case, the organization's members will be bound by them, eliminating the need to repeat them in the Engaged Team Charter. Teams can then express their interpretation or add complementary elements specific to their operations. For instance, although solidarity might not be a fundamental principle for the entire organization, a team may choose to include it in its own Engaged Team Charter.

Beyond values and imperatives, fundamental principles may include broader statements such as "Individual interest can never take precedence over collective, societal, or environmental interests."

The art lies in maintaining a limited set of fundamental principles. Consider the Ten Commandments—four govern man's relationship with God, whereas six organize human interactions (thou shalt not kill, thou shalt not steal, etc.). If six commandments sufficed to regulate civil society, 5–15 fundamental principles should adequately serve an organization.

These fundamental principles, once established and respected, protect the organization against deviation while ensuring team cohesion through a shared cultural foundation. As each team naturally has its own way of operating, expecting uniform behaviors across teams would be unrealistic. Instead, these vital minimum shared principles enable effective collaboration while preserving autonomy in areas that they do not cover.

This approach creates a robust framework that serves multiple purposes. It establishes consistent behavioral standards across all levels while providing clarity about everyone's rights and obligations. When conflicts arise or decisions need to be made, these principles serve as a reference point, ensuring alignment with organizational values. The framework allows teams to maintain their specific operational approaches while working within clear boundaries. Most importantly, it fosters cohesion between teams through shared principles without sacrificing the autonomy needed for effective team performance. The result is a well-designed collaboration system that strikes a balance between unity and flexibility.

5.1.1　Benefits of the Engaged Team Charter

The first two levels address the imperative of collective success, whereas the others focus on the imperatives of fairness and caring.

One key advantage of the Engaged Team Charter is its ability to mobilize all team members by aligning both their vision of collective success (through the first two rocket stages) and their interaction parameters. The final four rocket stages thus define the culture desired by team members.

When the group explicitly defines the rules, anyone unwilling to conform automatically places themselves at odds with the group. When there is incompatibility between the charter and a "dissenter's"[4] behavior, the dissenter has three fundamental options: change their behavior, convince the team to modify the charter at the next revision, or… leave the team.

The social-pressure dynamic is particularly powerful when the charter is defined by the entire team. When rules are imposed by the leader alone, social pressure does not come into play, and dissenters can easily engage in cat-and-mouse games with the leadership. It is simple to demonize a "bad" leader who implements new "unfavorable" rules, but it is far more challenging to criticize colleagues for choosing rules one disagrees with. Generally, dissenters prefer to find another team whose rules better align with their preferences.

I believe that a dissenter in a team is like sand in an engine—they impair performance. For the good of both the team and the dissenter, separation is often the best course of action. This separation need not be confrontational. Ending an incompatibility can be an excellent way of correcting a casting error or just improving the work climate.

The reality is that each of us connects more closely with some people than with others. We must accept that "chemistry" might not work between certain individuals, and there is no shame in being incompatible. As in a romantic relationship, separation is often the simplest solution. When we accept that separation can be beneficial and that incompatibility is not anyone's fault, the parting can remain cordial.

One of the Engaged Team Charter's strengths is its ability to objectify separation by highlighting the incompatibility between the dissenter and the group's chosen charter. When a leader imposes the rules, the conflict becomes a clash between two individual viewpoints, making both parties more likely to spiral into conflict. In this way, the Engaged Team Charter promotes group hygiene.

Ultimately, articulating the charter's six pillars means explicitly defining the team's desired culture, as opposed to the implicit, inherited culture. This process provides an opportunity to evolve team culture in the desired direction.

5.1.2   The Engaged Team Charter Significantly Improves Recruitment

When a new hire joins the group, it is like introducing a foreign body—this "transplant" activates the group's immune system, which can either accept or reject the graft. Hiring incompatible individuals is like setting a time bomb: sooner or

---

[4]This term carries here no pejorative or political connotation and it contains no judgment. It just means that the person in question opposes the governance system in place, which in this case has been adopted by the group.

later, it will explode. To prevent an explosion or rejection, ensure that new hires are compatible with the existing team culture.

The Engaged Team Charter enables frank discussions with candidates about these crucial compatibility issues. You can ask them directly if they believe that they are compatible with the team culture described in the charter. Their confirmation of compatibility becomes a commitment that serves as a reference point should they later transgress. Having been warned and having confirmed their agreement to respect these rules, they can no longer claim ignorance.

Implementing an Engaged Team Charter reduces the risk of time bombs in your team. Without a charter that explicitly states the rules of engagement, newcomers who have not been properly informed can easily take refuge behind the excuse that they were not told everything when they were hired.

By improving recruitment alignment, the charter also enhances retention. Those who feel comfortable and protected by the framework defined in the charter will be more likely to stay with the organization. The clarity provided by the charter helps to create a stable, cohesive team environment where everyone understands and accepts the operating principles.

In Practice

The proposed approach can be implemented at an organization-wide level, but it works best when started with small individual teams. Implementing across an entire organization is more challenging, so it is more practical to begin with one or several small teams.

Here is the implementation mechanism that I use:

1. All team members discuss the content of the six rocket levels. If the entire team cannot meet at the same time, arrange alternative discussion methods.
2. Document the consensus results in the Engaged Team Charter.
3. Submit the Engaged Team Charter for approval to the team leader's superior. This ensures that nothing contradicts the organization's fundamental principles, whether formally documented or implicit.
4. Publish and enforce the Engaged Team Charter.
5. Use the Engaged Team Charter during the recruitment process to invite candidates to evaluate and confirm their willingness to comply—even before the first interview (why interview incompatible candidates?). This helps to anticipate behavioral compatibility and better manage expectations.

As perfectly formalizing the six pillars on the first attempt is challenging, plan for periodic charter reviews. A stable governance structure typically emerges only after several iterations. It is advisable to establish an update mechanism in advance, either periodic or triggered when dysfunction requires adjustment.

5.1.3 A Final Critical Recommendation for Creating Your First Engaged Team Charter

Experience demonstrates that team charters developed without an external facilitator rarely match the effectiveness of those guided by a neutral, external party. The main advantage of bringing in an outsider is their ability to address sensitive topics without suspicion of manipulation. They can also challenge appealing but ultimately impractical ideas.

Some leaders make the mistake of creating their Engaged Team Charter alone, without external facilitation.

The only scenarios where leader-led facilitation works are when all team members feel completely safe expressing their thoughts without fear of consequences. As such ideal cases are rare, people seldom speak freely during charter discussions. Unfortunately, a charter led by a leader who controls the process will typically not accurately reflect the team's genuine desires.

When in doubt, the simplest solution is to anonymously ask the team if they prefer an external facilitator. If they feel safer with a neutral facilitator, but the leader proceeds to facilitate anyway, it becomes a token exercise that will not achieve the desired results.

Based on my experience, the initial Engaged Team Charter benefits significantly from external facilitation. However, subsequent updates can be managed by any team member, including the leader, provided that trust levels are sufficiently high (which can be measured).

In Practice

When I serve as an external facilitator, I add some preliminary steps to the process described earlier:

A. Initial Presentation: I explain the underlying logic of the Engaged Team Charter to all participants invited to define it. This 90-min presentation, either in-person or remote, establishes a foundation for understanding.

B. Online Survey: I ask each team member, including the leader, to complete an online survey to better understand their desired team culture. Having attended the presentation (A), they better comprehend the purpose of each question. As I am the only one who sees their responses and they trust my confidentiality, they express themselves freely without fear of repercussions or retaliation.

C. Draft Development and Review: based on survey responses and my experience, I create an initial charter draft.

D. Verification: I discuss the draft with the team manager to ensure content acceptability and their willingness to comply. In my experience, significant modifications due to leader objections are rare.

E. Team Discussion: we then proceed to debate the draft charter's content with the entire team (as explained in point 1 above).

The major advantage of discussing a prewritten draft is efficiency—charter adoption typically occurs within one day. Starting from a blank page without a first draft significantly extends the duration of the debate.

Even when well-intentioned managers draft the charter themselves, they often face inherent suspicion of manipulation. An external facilitator who has earned respondents' trust avoids this leadership-position handicap.

Although engaging an external facilitator involves costs, the investment is quickly offset by the superior quality of the resulting charter, leading to better team harmony and smoother operations.

The facilitator does not need to be external to the organization. They can come from another unit within the organization. The crucial requirement is that team members and their managers perceive them as neutral.

Before beginning the charter development process:

- Use anonymous surveys[5] to gauge team preference for external versus internal facilitation
- Ensure psychological safety throughout the charter development process
- Select facilitators with proven experience in team charter development
- Plan for regular charter reviews and updates once trust is established

5.1.4   Example of an Engaged Team Charter

The following generic example comes from a training center within an organization. Each of the six levels contains only selected content to illustrate the approach, particularly regarding expected behaviors. To avoid listing all behaviors and ensure that they reflect the team's specific personality and culture, only key examples are mentioned.

Excerpts illustrating the content of an Engaged Team Charter

- **Training Center Team Finality**
  Develop our colleagues' employability.
- To achieve this, we must:
  – Anticipate, design, coordinate, and deploy training actions aligned with strategy and both individual and collective needs

---

[5] EazyMirror at www.EazyMirror.com is a simple and cost-effective way of finding out team preferences thanks to its low cost customizable surveys.

- Ensure promotion and visibility of training actions to inspire personal-development desires
- Inform, raise awareness, guide/advise, and encourage colleagues regarding skills and personal development
- **Key Indicators of Success**
  - How much do employees believe that the training center helps to develop their employability?
  - How much does management believe that the training center contributes to strategy deployment?
  - How engaged are training-center employees?
- **Team Imperatives** (in order of priority)

  1. Collective success
  2. Fairness
  3. Caring
  4. Solidarity
  5. Transparency

- **Expected Behaviors Among Team Members**
  - *Professionalism*
    Demonstrate rigor
    Follow through on commitments
    Proactively suggest improvements
    Show proactive learning desire, curiosity, and open-mindedness
    Encourage and accept questioning
    Update knowledge and pursue improvement
    Acknowledge, learn from, and correct mistakes
    Avoid rushing without complete information
    Show discernment in priorities and processes
  - *Feedback*
    Address both areas for improvement and recognition of success
    Provide caring, constructive feedback promptly, within seven working days; do not accumulate grievances
    Keep feedback factual, focused on observed behaviors, never personal
    Receive feedback as a gift for improvement
    Accept feedback without arguing or justifying
  - *Team Spirit*
    Consider divergent opinions
    Communicate information and challenges
    Acknowledge limitations/strengths and seek support
    Practice collegial decision-making
    Ask for judgment-free help
    Quickly defuse conflicts through discussion/negotiation/explanation
    Share knowledge, information, and experiences
    Include and consider all members (including newcomers)
    No finger-pointing or disparagement
    Welcome and train newcomers or visitors with care

- *Expected Manager Behaviors*
  Consider team opinions before deciding (except in crises)
  Remain open to suggestions
  Encourage initiative
  Avoid micromanagement
  Defend the team
  Enforce the charter without compromise
  Clearly communicate organizational strategy
- **Governance Rules**
  - No privileges: charter applies to everyone
  - Zero tolerance for toxic behavior
  - Promote only those with required competencies
  - Good-faith mistakes are not punished
  - Internal candidates have priority for open positions
- **Protection Measures**

  - Regularly evaluate charter compliance using EazyMirror.com
  - Charter violations must have consequences
  - Consequences proportional to severity, up to team exclusion
  - Management must enforce the charter
  - Communicate consequences while protecting individuals when possible
  - Any team member can request arbitration from X^6 in case of disagreement

5.1.5   Additional Tools for Promoting Collective Success

The Engaged Team Charter includes three essential governance components:

- Explicitly stating your team's finality/purpose[7]
- Carefully selecting indicators to measure how well the agreed-upon purpose is being achieved[8]
- Ensuring that expected team behaviors support both collective success and, most importantly, well-being[9]

For best results, these three previously discussed pillars of collective success should be complemented by those that follow.

---

[6] Where X is the designated "wise counsel" who is not part of the team but has been chosen by the training center team members to arbitrate potential disagreements.

[7] Lever 37.

[8] Lever 38.

[9] Lever 54.

Lever 39 • Deploy Management by Opportunity (MbOp) to innovate

In today's world, "innovation" often means "projects." All enlightened leaders understand that the world is changing, and innovation is imperative for survival. No industry's business model remains unchallenged. Waves of technological and business disruption are crashing into industries one after another, demanding constant adaptation and resilience. From postal services to medicine to banking, these transformative forces will spare no one, particularly because of:

* Digital transformation powered by the enormous impact of artificial intelligence, automation, and blockchain
* Smart robots
* The enormous impact on industry of 3D printing
* Life sciences development
* New business models riding these waves of change

Assuming that your activity or industry will be immune to disruption is a dangerous form of complacency. As salvation can only come through innovation, no organization can ensure its sustainability without innovating.

I find it telling that although 96% of executives consider creativity integral to their business, only 23% believe that they have succeeded in demonstrating it.[10] This poor result reflects two major challenges: the difficulty of balancing innovation with daily operations, and the failure of traditional innovation management approaches in established companies.

To overcome these challenges, I believe that it is indispensable to understand the barriers that prevent organizations from innovating more successfully. Having addressed this question in detail in my article in *Expansion Management Review*,[11] I focus here on the essential points.

The first barrier I have observed lies in leadership's attitude. Some leaders fear changing successful formulas, hoping that current success continues. This faith in the status quo acts as "Innovation Botox"—paralyzing progress. Relying on proven recipes and operational excellence prevents leaders from encouraging their staff to come up with innovative ideas or explore new avenues.

The second barrier I have identified stems from leadership style. Some leaders restrict innovation to a select few. Suffering from the "Not Invented Here" syndrome, often coupled with superiority complexes, these leaders dismiss the ideas of others. They believe that their supposedly superior innovation capabilities justify their higher remuneration. This approach deprives organizations of insights from frontline employees who encounter opportunities daily—opportunities that R&D researchers and managers, isolated from the field, often cannot even imagine. Your attitude toward innovation will inevitably impact your employees' level of engagement.

---

[10] Ruth Mortimer, "Turn Creativity into Strategy for Success," Marketing Week, 16 July 2009.

[11] "Libérer l'inventivité dans les entreprises," Expansion Management Review, September 2008.

I have seen how leaders who take the opposite approach, as demonstrated by the example of Google, reap extraordinary benefits. By encouraging their employees to propose initiatives, they tap into an extraordinary reservoir of creativity. This illustrates a key distinction between management and leadership: while management focuses on implementing plans and processes, leadership inspires people to pursue excellence and contribute to competitive advantage. Encouraging people to innovate impacts their level of engagement.

The third barrier I have encountered comes from inadequate framework conditions. Organizational structure should not stifle initiatives. Instead, you need systems that encourage innovation through rewards for competitive advantages, streamlined administrative procedures, and extraordinary budgets for unpredictable innovative projects.

The fourth barrier I have identified manifests in the implementation gap. Although employees have numerous ideas, very few are implemented. The absence of structured methods for evaluating ideas and presenting them convincingly to decision-makers creates a major handicap. In my experience with the IpOp model,[12] I have observed that 33–56 percent of employees trained in this approach launch innovative projects that they would not have considered before discovering this methodology for bringing ideas to life.

In Practice

This analysis of innovation barriers naturally leads to identifying measures to stimulate it. Each barrier corresponds to a pillar supporting innovation. These four pillars are formalized in "Management by Opportunities" (MbOp).[13]

The first pillar concerns the leadership engagement level. How you welcome innovations presented to you will determine the perception of your caring attitude and your commitment to supporting collective success. The three other innovation pillars often depend heavily on the leadership engagement level. Therefore, implementing them represents a managerial act of good governance.

The second pillar, concerning leadership methods, is the subject of this book. A fair and caring leader who applies the principles outlined in this book will naturally be inclined to support innovation. Being caring and wanting to ensure the organization's sustainability, you cannot help but welcome favorably any initiative that may contribute to it. Similarly, you will implement the third and fourth pillars to promote employee contribution to collective success and reward them fairly. A virtuous circle will quickly be established.

---

[12] The IpOp Model is a structured approach to evaluating, selecting, and implementing innovative ideas. For more information, see: R. H Cohen, *Pre-project excellence: Unleashing the Power of IpOp Model and ISO 56007 for Superior Project Outcomes and Selection*, Springer, 2024; and https://en.wikipedia.org/wiki/IpOp_Model.

[13] MbOp is described in Chapter 22 of: R. H Cohen, *Pre-project excellence: Unleashing the Power of IpOp Model and ISO 56007 for Superior Project Outcomes and Selection*, Springer, 2024.

The third pillar, dealing with framework conditions, has been extensively covered in management literature dedicated to intrapreneurship. Reflections on this theme primarily focus on systems to promote innovation, assuming that once systems are in place, expected results will follow. As reality unfortunately does not correspond to this determinism, innovation results rarely meet expectations. This may explain why this theme is less popular. Without disparaging them, it seems more realistic to consider that implementing framework conditions is not the sole miracle solution but one required component of it.

The fourth pillar provides employees with the tools that they need to transform ideas into reality. This pillar is essential because if no one can implement an idea, the other three pillars remain ineffective. Unfortunately, most organizations rely on their employees' pre-existing know-how for this phase. Yet, this transition from idea to action is far from being properly internalized, meaning that people with these skills represent only a small minority. As many companies associate innovation with creativity, most internal training efforts focus on creativity (lateral thinking, "out of the box" thinking, etc.). Although creativity contributes to innovation, it is far from sufficient. True innovation—the kind that creates value—exists only when put into action. To take action, tools are needed.

Fortunately, more tools are being taught and used, including design thinking, lean innovation, fast-prototyping, business model canvas, incubators that guide potential innovators, etc. All of these are useful and relevant for some issues that innovators must address. However, they lack an overall approach that allows consideration of all parameters affecting the fate of an innovation or a project. To avoid missing parameters that could influence the final success, you need a holistic approach, one that considers not just questions about customers or business models. Among the tools offering a holistic approach is the IpOp model, which has inspired the ISO 56007 standard (Tools and methods for managing opportunities and ideas—Guidance).[14] Whatever the approach, keep in mind that, given project complexity, it is imperative to use tools that consider all key success factors, including stakeholders, rather than just a few, as is almost always the case except with the IpOp Model. Beware of missing the forest for the trees!

As your relationship with opportunities and innovation is symptomatic of your dynamics and organizational culture, the governance you establish must also consider how innovation is managed. It should therefore create clear pathways for innovation. This means establishing transparent evaluation processes and

---

[14] See my book "Pre-project excellence: Unleashing the Power of IpOp Model and ISO 56007 for Superior Project Outcomes and Selection," which explains how to use the IpOp Model to deploy ISO 56007 best practices in real life.

providing resources for developing promising initiatives. By recognizing and rewarding innovative contributions, you foster an environment where experimentation is encouraged and new ideas can flourish.

Your level of receptivity to others' contributions reveals a great deal about your leadership. Through your daily actions, you demonstrate your openness to new ideas from all levels, your commitment to collective growth, and your trust in employees' capabilities.

Remember that receptivity to innovation demonstrates caring leadership in multiple ways. By acknowledging the value of each team member's perspective and supporting professional growth through innovation opportunities, you build trust through active listening and engagement. This approach contributes to the organization's long-term success while creating a culture where everyone feels empowered to contribute their ideas and insights.

Lever 40 • Encourage Constructive Questioning

One key to evolution lies in the ability to question things. Accepting without thinking maintains the status quo, whereas questioning drives the pursuit of better ways to do things. In innovation, questioning is essential and must be encouraged. This was one of the rules that Steve Jobs applied relentlessly.

The same question applies to challenging managerial practices, received instructions, or decisions made: should you encourage employees to question them? Based on my experience, encouraging questioning prevents employees from acting mindlessly. Once they understand the purpose of what needs to be done, it is better for them to consider adapting processes to circumstances. As it is impossible to anticipate everything in advance, there are always circumstances that require standard processes to be adapted.

Similarly, the infallible leader who knows everything does not exist. If such a person existed, everyone would know about it and compete to hire them. The reality is that we are all fallible and two minds are better than one. Encouraging questioning allows you to mobilize multiple minds instead of one. As it also recognizes your employees' capacity to contribute, encouraging them to do so is not only rewarding for them but also demonstrates caring. Moreover, as questioning improves vigilance against missteps, it proves highly useful.

The tragic example of the Challenger space shuttle (1986) illustrates this point. A NASA employee did not dare report that a seal might not withstand the new weather conditions imposed by the rocket-launch delay. The result was a dramatic explosion that cost seven astronauts their lives. This example has inspired much reflection on the necessity of speaking up and not showing blind submission to superiors. Many have demonstrated that servile obedience to leadership ultimately harms organizations in the long term.

The antidote to servile submission to positional power is daring to express doubts, articulate potential incompetence, and question what is commonly accepted, particularly regarding processes or even received instructions. The constructive questioning I am referring to is not meant to be done out of principle or in contradiction. Instead, the objective is to mobilize common sense to verify that what is prescribed will indeed achieve the desired result. The questioner's perception may prove inaccurate, but what matters is engaging in debate, examining things thoroughly, and thus progressing.

For constructive questioning to be as beneficial as I describe, it must be well understood by all and not perceived as a form of rebellion or contestation. This presupposes making it, like feedback, a governance rule to include in the Engaged Team Charter.

Important: In Practice

For questioning to be effectively constructive, several essential conditions must be met. Your employees must feel safe expressing themselves openly without fear of repercussions. This psychological safety forms the foundation of honest dialogue and meaningful improvement.

Questioning should always be conducted with respect, challenging ideas rather than individuals. The focus must remain on concepts, processes, and outcomes rather than turning into personal attacks. This approach maintains professional dignity while fostering productive discussion.

The process must consistently demonstrate caring and be aimed at promoting collective success. Every question raised should serve to improve team or organizational outcomes. This shared goal helps to maintain positive intent and a collaborative spirit.

Any refusal of suggested changes must always be backed by clear reasoning. When ideas or questions are not accepted, providing thorough explanations helps to maintain transparency and trust, ensuring that everyone understands the decision-making process.

As the ability to debate requires verbal and communication skills, you naturally benefit from surrounding yourself with people capable of expressing their doubts and raising concerns clearly. Their ability to frame questions constructively while maintaining respect helps to create an environment where meaningful dialogue can thrive, especially when dealing with complex challenges or sensitive topics. Team members who can articulate their thoughts effectively help to prevent misunderstandings and enable more efficient problem-solving.

Lever 41 • Select Projects with Rigor and Transparency

Project selection statistics reveal a concerning governance issue. Only 29% of I.T. projects are completed on time and within budget, whereas approximately 19% fail or are abandoned before reaching their objectives.[15] These statistics, which some consider optimistic despite their disappointing workplace experiences, clearly

---

[15] Standish Group CHAOS Report 2015.

demonstrate a governance problem in project selection. If projects were better evaluated before launch, fewer would likely be initiated. Although project abandonment cannot be avoided entirely, especially owing to changing circumstances, the 30% abandonment rate could be reduced through better upstream evaluation.

Poor project selection acts as organizational poison in two dramatic ways. First, it results in a genuine waste of resources that could have been better utilized elsewhere. Second, these projects unnecessarily consume employee energy. This energy could be directed toward worthier projects that build competitive advantages or contribute to success in other important ways. By burdening employees, poorly selected projects clearly contradict the imperative of collective success, which demands optimal use of time and resources.

Launching projects that should not be initiated demonstrates a lack of fairness and caring. The funds allocated to these projects could have been used to better compensate employees or to invest in the organization's long-term sustainability. Furthermore, poor project selection contradicts both the imperatives of collective success and the principles of caring and fairness.

Decision makers undermine their credibility through poor resource allocation choices. How can employees respect leaders who lack the discernment to correctly evaluate the merit of a project? How can they accept resource-request denials for their own projects, particularly when the argument is...a lack of resources?

While 84–88% of projects do not proceed as planned or hoped, decision makers should reasonably question what can be done to limit damage. A primary difficulty that they face is that project management methods such as PMI and Prince 2 offer excellent tools for implementing projects once launch decisions are made. Despite their qualities, these tools are not appropriate for the pre-project phase, when launch decisions are being made.

The essence of the problem lies in insufficiently formalized project evaluation criteria. A study showed that decision makers use between three and nine criteria to analyze a project, averaging six. Unfortunately, this is insufficient, as demonstrated by the latest version of the IpOp model,[16] which, in its decision tree included in ISO 56007 standard best practices, highlights the necessity of verifying at least 11 parameters. The gap between these 11 criteria and the small number used in practice during decision making means that decision makers yield to the temptation of reducing parameters, for simplification or, more precisely, to avoid complexity. As grasping complexity is laborious, focusing on a smaller number of parameters is very appealing.

The problem with this excessive simplification is that it inevitably leads to ignoring parameters that could affect project outcomes. With luck, one may slip through unscathed. Without luck, it is highly likely that one of the overlooked parameters will cause the project to stumble, derail or at least slow down or consume more resources than expected. This largely explains the aforementioned unflattering statistics on project success.

---

[16] See my book "Pre-project excellence: Unleashing the Power of IpOp Model and ISO 56007 for Superior Project Outcomes and Selection," op.cit.

Another certainty to keep in mind is that, on the roads, collisions never occur with identified obstacles, but with those not identified early enough to react accordingly. This is the logic of the blind spot in a car. To avoid it, we add mirrors: one in the center, one on the right, and another on the left. Someone who, for the sake of simplification, finds it too complex to monitor three mirrors simultaneously obviously puts themselves at a greater risk than someone willing to handle the complexity of monitoring all three.

Imagine the sense of security passengers would feel if a pilot announced that, for simplicity's sake, they were not using all their cockpit instruments! Yet, as business leaders are also pilots, with the heavy responsibility of making the best use of resources entrusted to them, they have the imperative duty to comprehend all parameters to understand the ins and outs of each project.

The trap that many leaders fall into is the "one-page syndrome." By requesting that each issue be summarized in a maximum of one page, they risk missing parameters that have a real influence on the course of events. Saving time is desirable, but because simplification is reductive, it prevents the complexity of things from being grasped. Unfortunately for leaders, a project is by definition... complex. Rushing project evaluation by oversimplifying is, therefore, a true governance crime.

To drive the point home and ensure that you do not fall into the trap of reductive simplifications, I paraphrase H.L. Mencken, who reminds us that "for every complex problem, there is one solution that is simple, clear, and... wrong."

This observation perfectly captures the danger of oversimplified project evaluation. When leaders look for quick, simple solutions to complex project challenges, they often overlook critical factors that could undermine success. The allure of simple answers must not override the necessity of thorough analysis. The cost of oversimplification ultimately proves far greater than the investment required for proper pre-project analysis.

In Practice

Given the aforementioned impact of poor pre-project analysis and project selection, more rigorous upstream analysis emerges as the solution that not only eliminates projects that should never have been launched but also better anticipates the cost and duration of those ultimately approved.

To implement effective project selection governance:

- Establish strict discipline for resource allocation to new projects
- Utilize the IpOp model's decision tree for comprehensive pre-project evaluation
- Document evaluation criteria and decision rationale
- Review selection effectiveness regularly
- Maintain consistent standards across all project proposals

Remember that the IpOp decision tree provides:

- Essential criteria for pre-project evaluation
- A structured approach to decision-making
- A clear framework for resource allocation
- A systematic review of critical success factors
- Tools for measuring project viability

5.2   Tools for Fairness

As indicated above, several essential governance points are part of the Engaged Team Charter:

- The need to clarify imperatives that each team wishes to follow on top of the fundamental principles of the organization[17]
- The explicit statement of governance rules[18]
- The importance of measures protecting those who respect the Engaged Team Charter[19]
- The mechanism for enforcing the Engaged Team Charter (internal justice system)[20]

Being demanding, I believe it is necessary to refine these points or complement them with the following additional elements to consider in governance.

Lever 46 • Ensure that the Dignity of Each Person Is Respected

This necessity, addressed in Chap. 2, needs no further elaboration. I want to emphasize that this governance rule represents an essential lever that supports both fairness and caring.

In Practice

To implement this governance rule effectively:

- Make dignity protection a fundamental principle of the organization
- Create clear protocols for addressing dignity violations
- Establish feedback mechanisms for reporting concerns
- Ensure consistent application across all levels
- Monitor and measure compliance regularly

---

[17] See Lever 43.

[18] See Lever 44.

[19] See Lever 26.

[20] See Lever 45.

Lever 47 • Ensure that Everyone Is Accountable

Another essential team governance mechanism is ensuring team members understand that they are accountable.

"Accountability" ensures that everyone faces the consequences of their actions or inactions. It means, in a way, accepting these consequences. Without it, less conscientious individuals are encouraged to slack off. As not everyone in society is necessarily conscientious, it is in your interest to define the rules of the game. This framework is precisely what governance addresses.

Once a team culture incorporates accountability, members become reliable and fulfill their responsibilities. Everyone knows that they can count on each colleague, barring unforeseen circumstances. Without accountability, people must chase after deliverables, verify that promises will be kept on time, follow up repeatedly, extend their own deadlines because they have not received what they expected, and so forth. All of this consumes time and represents multiple grains of sand that slow down the team's collective performance.

The lack of accountability inevitably leads to dysfunctions that can only negatively impact collective success. Eventually, this inefficiency may even affect the sustainability of the team or organization, which will be supplanted by more effective ones.

Allowing people who do not fulfill their commitments to escape consequences amounts to a lack of fairness. Therefore, failing to establish a culture of accountability is essentially an invitation to transgress the "fairness" imperative. If those who transgress face no consequences, why would others play the fool by doing everything correctly? To avoid sanctions, it becomes much easier to do the minimum required. This inevitably leads to decreased collective performance. As the cost of a lack of accountability is very high for the organization, making accountability a core principle at the governance level is an unavoidable necessity.

Being accountable means accepting the consequences of not honoring a commitment. This commitment could involve doing one's job properly, completing tasks within the agreed timeframe, transmitting information to those who need it, behaving appropriately, and so on.

In Practice

Having accountability presupposes an evaluation, whatever its form, of:

- What people do but should not do
- What they do not do but should do

This evaluation requires wisdom on your part—not only the discernment to distinguish between situations, but also the courage to take action.

Once you observe failures from those who do not honor their commitments, you inevitably come to appreciate those who honor and do the right thing. This awareness leads to recognizing their contribution to collective success and acknowledging it. As recognition is one of the least well-satisfied expectations among employees, despite being at the heart of fairness, it remains one of the main sources of frustration/dissatisfaction expressed by employees. As stated in Lever 11, no fair and caring leader can afford the luxury of ignoring recognition, nor the need to enforce accountability.

By establishing an accountability mechanism, you significantly promote the development of a culture where recognition has the place it deserves. You also prevent slackers from dragging the team down.

Without this rigor, your credibility will take a hit: what respect can you hope for from employees who see that you let slackers get away with it? No courage, no respect!

Thus, when governance includes accountability requirements, you automatically establish a virtuous circle that prevents many of the perverse situations that undermine employee trust.

Nobody's Fault
Once upon a time there were four people named Everybody, Somebody, Anybody, and Nobody.
There was an important job to do, and Everybody was asked to do it.
Everybody was convinced that Somebody would do it.
Anybody could have done it, but in reality, Nobody did.
Somebody got angry because it was Everybody's job!
Everybody thought that Anybody could do it.
And Nobody doubted that Somebody would do it.
In the end, Everybody blamed Anybody,
because Nobody did what Somebody could have done.

Moral of the Story
Without blaming Everybody, it would be best if Everybody did what they are supposed to do, without hoping that Somebody will do it in their place. Experience shows that where Somebody is expected, one generally finds Nobody.
[Source unknown]

Accountable leaders should always provide clear, comprehensive, and transparent reasons for approving or rejecting projects or innovations, with no hidden agenda. In this section on fairness and up to this point, I have primarily emphasized honoring commitments. However, there is another dimension that complements what has already been said: the necessity to transparently justify what is decided or done.

The consequences of lack of transparency in decision-making

Here is an interesting example illustrating my point, one that is very common in organizations: Michael submits an innovative project to his manager, John, but John dismisses it using an unconvincing pretext. What happened? Among the reasons that led John to eliminate Michael's proposal, we can imagine that:

- John fears that implementing this project could impose additional effort that he does not want to undertake.
- If the idea led to failure, someone might blame John for supporting a bad project. However, if nothing happens, no one will criticize him. This is often what occurs in the absence of a right to fail. It maintains a finger-pointing culture, also known as a blame culture, which stigmatizes people who have supported initiatives that fail, even though this happens to the best of us. This culture naturally transforms managers into naysayers, those who always say no. Because they have too little to gain by saying yes and nothing to lose by saying no, they become innovation killers.
- This project could encroach on the territory of other managers. To avoid an unpleasant confrontation, John prefers not to get involved.
- This project would have no impact on the promotion John hopes to receive for his own career.
- This project, which could be very relevant for the company, would not contribute to achieving the personal objectives John needs to obtain his bonus.

All these excuses drawn from real life have several things in common. First, they are bad and would be poorly received by John's superiors if they knew about them. Moreover, they are not transparent at all, because to avoid developing them, John will have resorted to another pretext to kill the idea. Notably that the same idea has already been considered and rejected in the past, that the timing is not right, that it is too different from what made past success possible, and so on. Since all these bad pretexts rest on statements that are generally difficult to verify, they exempt John from explaining his decision to kill Michael's idea. John's decision, whose real reason cannot be admitted, thus contains an arbitrary element that makes it practically a minor abuse of power, too discreet to be noticed.

In practice, and since supporting Michael's project will require an allocation of resources, this allocation will be examined with much more attention than the decision to abandon it. In case of abandonment, no one will ask John for explanations. There is thus an obvious imbalance of attention between the yes to a project that consumes resources, such as time and money, and the incognito no that mobilizes no resources and about which no one is informed.

In an environment or culture in which it is established that everyone is accountable, the rejection of a project or its approval requires explanations. This presupposes that the criteria for accepting and rejecting projects are known and transparent, as is the case with the IpOp Model decision tree mentioned earlier.

Justifying your decisions is part of being accountable. This mitigates the possibilities of abuse of power or arbitrariness. Being accountable with full transparency promotes the operationalization of fairness. I even suspect that it is indispensable to fairness.

5.3   Tools for Caring Leadership

Lever 48 • Enforce the "No Asshole Rule"

When discussing professional relationships, we inevitably talk about "assholes," as described by Robert Sutton in his book "The No Asshole Rule."[21] I love this book's title because it legitimizes the use of this vocabulary. The author explains the catastrophic impact "assholes" have on organizations, particularly in terms of decreased performance. As the presence of such a person drives away talent and destroys the engagement level of those subjected to their behavior, the recommended solution is to introduce the... "No Asshole Rule." Banning assholes is easy to say but more difficult to enforce.

These individuals generally offer enough value to the company that leaders turn a blind eye to their toxicity. They might be the irreplaceable expert or the super salesperson. If they were not performing, they would have been ejected long ago. As replacing them is painful, the temptation to accommodate them can be hard to resist. Separating from them requires courage, but you must also keep in mind that, as Robert Sutton explains, the departure of the "asshole" will be largely compensated by the increased performance of those who were demotivated by their behavior. Removing them is like extracting a wisdom tooth—it hurts in the moment, but once it is done, you live much better and more happily.

I especially want to emphasize that tolerating "assholes" means lacking caring toward all their victims. It goes without saying that the Fair and Caring leader's toolkit must include the "No Asshole Rule". In my eyes, this rule, aimed at protecting employees, should be a part of any Engaged Team's Charter.

For those who cringe at the term "asshole," I suggest an alternative terminology: "the No-Incompatible-Team-Member Rule." Anyone who deliberately or simply, through disinterest, fails to respect the content of the Engaged Team Charter adopted by all members is considered... incompatible. The

---

[21] Robert Sutton, op. cit.

benefit of this perspective is that incompatibility is not attributable to antipathy or abuse of power. Incompatibility is objective: comparing the incompatible person's behavior with those defined by the Engaged Team Charter highlights the incompatibility.

Whether it is the "No Asshole Rule" or the "No-Incompatible-Team-Member Rule," these rules remind us that:

1. **Compatible members deliver better results than those who are not.** The absence of compatibility corresponds to grains of sand that jam collaboration: when some team members are not pulling the rope in the same direction, the cumulative force is not optimal. To maximize performance, it is in the interest of shareholders and leaders to have compatible teams. It is also in the teams' interest because interactions are much more fluid and pleasant.

2. **Contrary to a commonly expressed misconception, one should not expect a manager** to successfully lead every type of person and simultaneously maximize team performance. If the team contains incompatible people, the tensions caused by incompatibility will inevitably result in lower performance. To allow the manager to optimize performance, you must permit them to separate from incompatible individuals.

3. **For incompatibility not to be perceived as arbitrary or an abuse of power,** it must be objectively demonstrable. One of the purposes of the Engaged Team Charter is precisely to objectify compatibility and, consequently, incompatibility.

4. **Compatibility does not imply the absence of diversity;** it simply requires agreement to respect the rules established in the Engaged Team Charter. Those who are unwilling to respect them are not compatible with the rest of the team.

5. **If everyone were compatible with one another, we would know it,** and everyone would be friends with everyone. We must therefore accept incompatibility as an unavoidable reality. As incompatibility is not a flaw and everyone has the right to live according to their beliefs and worldview, recognizing incompatibility should not lead to conflict. Separating from an incompatible person can therefore be done in a caring and respectful manner without reproach.

6. **Apply the "No-*Incompatible-Team-Member* Rule" with rigor, courage, and firmness.** The obvious conclusion from the above is that if you force yourself or, worse, accept being forced to keep incompatible people on your teams, you will face programmed failure. In the name of both performance and the well-being of your teams (which is a manifestation of caring), as well as your own well-being, separate yourself from incompatible individuals, but do it with respect and in a caring manner.

In Practice

One of the other benefits of "The No Asshole Rule" book is that it makes a great gift! This is an act of caring not only toward the victims of the "asshole" and for the unit where they operate, but also for the "asshole" themselves. Indeed, the book can help them to realize how they are perceived. It is a way of giving them feedback...

Robert Sutton explains that among those he calls "certified" assholes, some are unaware of their behavior and when they realize it, make efforts to change. Unfortunately, some do not care and have no intention of evolving. For the latter, the only solution for the organization is to eliminate them. Offering them the book is then not feedback but a warning...

Helping the first category to evolve is, therefore, an act of caring. But beware: offering them this book might be perceived as a rather uncaring act! Everything depends on how you approach it... Offering it by saying, "As this book made me reflect and encouraged me to change certain practices, I thought it might interest you too" would not be perceived in the same way as "you would benefit from reading this book"!

If, after reading, the person directly asks you "did you give it to me because you think I am an asshole?", you can respond with a simple "yes" or, in a more caring manner, "I have observed some behaviors that unfortunately work against you and that may lead certain people to draw conclusions that would be damaging. If you want examples, we can talk about it whenever you want."

Lever 49 • Apply "Fair Process"

This concept is based on the observation that stakeholders' acceptance of a decision or approach depends essentially on their understanding of the why and their perception that it is the best decision for a good cause. People are more than happy to let someone make the final decision, provided that they understand why that decision was made and that it was the best decision for the best reasons. To verify fairness, they observe how the decision was made and communicated.

In Fair and Caring leadership, the question of fairness is clearly central. As discussed above, it is reasonable to believe that when people understand the reasoning behind a decision, they are more likely to view it as just and fair. Acceptability, therefore, depends on people's perception of how you reached the decision: a fair process often matters more than the outcome itself!

This does not mean that everything must be handled in a participative manner by systematically involving people. Even if inclusiveness sometimes promotes acceptability, it is not a necessity. People may truly believe that a dictator is best positioned to make sound decisions. If they accept the dictator based on the acceptability criteria mentioned earlier, then the dictator's decisions will be well accepted.

As a Fair and Caring leader, you must ensure that the feeling of fairness is maintained. To achieve this, you must pay at least as much attention to how things are done as to the result to be obtained.

In Practice

To illustrate this point, let us take the example of the annual performance review, for which I will present two scenarios. By combining individually minor details, I have deliberately exaggerated to show how each small detail can contribute to escalating tension during a routine conversation with an employee.

Scenario 1: During the appointment, you rush to finish the interview because you know that several will follow throughout the day, and HR requires you to return the duly completed forms for all your team members by this evening. Moreover, you must attend your son's Christmas show where he plays guitar at 5 PM. The interview taking place in your office is interrupted by two client calls, and, for confidentiality reasons, you are annoyed that the employee whose annual evaluation you are conducting hears what you tell them. You sign two urgent letters that your assistant brings to you during the conversation. As you want to move quickly, it is mainly you who speaks and, to make the employee feel valued, you give them a good overall evaluation. It is a way of buying peace of mind. As the interview only lasts 20 min, you get off easily, and the employee who receives a good evaluation should be happy. Mission accomplished!

Scenario 2: You have organized the interview in the meeting room of another building, instructing your assistant not to disturb you. Before coming, you prepared a list of the collaborator's achievements for which you would like to congratulate them, and a list of skills that they would benefit from improving. During the interview, you listen carefully to how the collaborator perceives their performance and what they would like to improve. You realize that only one of the two improvement points that they envision coincides with yours, but as you sense that they are very motivated, you set aside the other point that they did not include in their list, planning to revisit it in a few months, once they have progressed on the point for which they are motivated. You discuss in detail their successes as well as the difficulties that they encounter and paths for improvement, including the role you could personally play to help them grow. You agree, ultimately, that certain sections of the form deserve a very good assessment and that three points require attention for improvement. An action plan is also agreed upon. After reviewing the collaborator's situation, you also asked for feedback on how things are going and their expectations regarding your behavior. The interview lasts one hour and thirty minutes, but you were able to verify that this collaborator demonstrates a high level of engagement, and you know what they expect from you for the next 6 months. The interview was useful for both them and you.

Without devoting time to a detailed analysis of the characteristics of each scenario, it is clear that the employee in scenario 2 appreciates their interview much more than the one in scenario 1, even though the first resulted in a better overall evaluation.

In both scenarios, it was a performance review: the "what" is the same. The difference lies in the process, the way it was handled. In scenario 2, the collaborator perceives that you demonstrate a sincere interest in their development, whereas in scenario 1, it is evident that the interview is viewed as a formality, not to say a... necessary evil.

This example highlights the importance of process over outcomes. The spirit of fair process consists of caring about how things are conducted to ensure that the perception of those involved remains as positive as possible. It is a manifestation of caring.

Another example is the process of building the Engaged Team Charter, as described earlier. When employees decide on its content after open discussion, the charter will be seen as legitimate. Regardless of whether the content is ideal, the way it is created is paramount. If everyone approves of the process, there will be no dispute.

Similarly, if an internal justice system is established with the agreement of all protagonists, the decisions made will be accepted, regardless of what they may be.

Lever 6 • Ask Yourself the Leader's Eight Questions

Understanding the necessity of a fair process is easy. Embodying it is another matter entirely. It requires constant vigilance because everything you do or say will be consciously or unconsciously evaluated by your team members to verify if it aligns with their perception of what is right. They do this reflexively, as an essential modality of their survival instinct. As explained in Chap. 1, humans are constantly on guard to identify signals announcing a threat. The observed absence of a fair process potentially recurring is a warning sign of future danger. Therefore, to ensure their survival, your team members are constantly on the lookout for any noncompliance with the fair process. As they will not forgive any failure and since their perception will influence their level of engagement, you have little choice.

In Practice

To find an effective approach (fair process), based on my experience, I invite you to systematically ask yourself the following eight questions (before deciding or acting!).

1. What will be the impact of what will be done/decided on the level of engagement and motivation of your employees?
2. Could your employees feel that their dignity will be wounded?

3. Will your employees feel they have been actually heard? This does not mean that you must do what they say, but it is important that their views have been heard and taken into account, to the extent possible.
4. Given the approach that will be used, what will their perception of fairness be?
5. Will they feel that things have been done with caring?
6. Once confronted with the decision, what will their emotions/feelings be?
7. How will the trust that they place in you be impacted by what will be done/decided?
8. What other approaches might better align the interest of your employees with yours and that of the team?

In reality, the first question is the most central. It is the one that you cannot afford to ignore. The next six are parameters that will influence the first, namely the level of engagement you generate. The eighth question is an invitation to explore alternative approaches to avoid rushing headlong into a wall. These questions should help you to avoid actions or decisions that would sabotage the level of engagement of your teams and, incidentally, your credibility. Your ability to embody a fair process will very likely influence your ability to mobilize teams, to succeed and, incidentally, your career...

Lever 50 • Generalize Frequent Caring Feedback

Feedback is a classic in the manager's toolkit. There is indeed a plethora of courses, seminars, workshops, etc., that explain, more or less effectively to managers, how to give feedback. I will highlight a few points that seem important to me but are not always well understood.

5.3.1   Hygiene Means 360° Feedback

Feedback is not just a tool for correction or an opportunity to explain to an employee what they could improve and, ideally, how to do so. It is much more than an alignment with a prescribed way of doing things. When properly understood and used, feedback is at the heart of a team's relational hygiene. "GE even replaced formal interviews in 2016 across all its entities with a continuous dialogue approach."[22]

To avoid any misunderstanding, I specify what feedback is or should be: giving a person negative or positive information about their behavior, which they may not be aware of, with the hope that this knowledge will be useful to them. By its very nature and because it is aimed at serving the other, feedback is an act of caring. It targets the interest of the other. Being only constructive, it corresponds to a gift for the one who receives information for their own good.

---

[22] Philippe Rodet and Yves Desjacques, op. cit.

When feedback is given solely to put an employee back on track because their manager wants things done in a certain way, this so-called feedback no longer targets the employee's interest but supports that of their manager. It is no longer caring but self-interested. It is no longer feedback but alignment with a prescribed norm or process.

One-directional feedback—meaning feedback that flows only from top to bottom—distorts the concept of feedback.

There is no contraindication for an employee to provide feedback to their leader. On the contrary, they should feel safe and confident enough to do so spontaneously and naturally. If the leader is not ready to accept it from their direct reports, it is likely because they have locked themselves into a myth of omnipotence and infallibility. This form of arrogance necessarily weakens their ability to lead. Feedback should be omnidirectional and part of a culture that promotes the exchange of useful information, regardless of hierarchical level.

For omnidirectional feedback to be possible, there are essential prerequisites:

- **A relationship of trust** (back to square one: see Chap. 2) **and a sense of psychological safety**. Without these, fear inevitably arises, preventing open communication. The moment that someone is afraid to speak up, it means that this person does not feel confident enough, or worse, not safe.
- **Training everyone in the organization on how to give and receive feedback.** Because giving feedback is understood as an important skill that managers should master, most trainings focus on giving feedback while targeting managers. This is a gross error: because it is also difficult to receive feedback, it is imperative to train both the giver and the receiver. This implies training every single employee in giving and receiving feedback. It also ensures that feedback is not only top–down but 360°. Everyone in the organization should be allowed—and obviously trained—to give feedback to anyone else.

In Practice

A team's life is filled with micro-events or interactions that can be awkward,[23] misinterpreted,[24] poorly communicated, poorly experienced, and more. These micro-frustrations are like small abscesses that pollute the relationship. If the "frustrated" person speaks up, the person causing the frustration has the opportunity to:

- Dispel any possible misunderstanding that led to an inaccurate perception by the frustrated person

---

[23] Anyone can, at one time or another be awkward.

[24] Everyone sees things according to their own filters.

- Explain what was misunderstood or misinterpreted and thus change the perception of the frustrated person
- Realize the impact of what was said/done to say/do differently in the future
- Apologize by acknowledging any possible awkwardness.

Lancing these abscesses is as essential to relational hygiene as brushing your teeth. Fortunately, the frequency of feedback is not twice a day. I have found that a weekly or bi-weekly rhythm generally works very well.

This periodic debriefing point should, of course, be scheduled. Its necessity and modalities also benefit from being made explicit in the Engaged Team Charter, not only regarding business issues but also everything related to relationships.

In an ideal world, the Engaged Team Charter should anticipate all possible situations to codify them. As this ideal world does not exist, no charter can be exhaustive enough to cover all possibilities. There remain unforeseen situations that, like a pebble in a shoe, can be described as "irritating." As a result, adjustments and clarifications must be made along the way for all relational irritants.

The institutionalization of continuous, caring feedback serves as a safety valve that helps to address the inevitable gaps in the Engaged Team Charter. Feedback makes it possible to address any "irritants" that the charter has not resolved clearly enough. It also provides an opportunity to recognize when certain provisions of the charter are not achieving the desired results and to consider modifications during the next revision.

5.3.2   On the Proper Use of Feedback

Many managers mistakenly believe that feedback is primarily an opportunity to point out what their team members need to change. As a result, feedback is often seen as a tool for enforcing alignment or driving compliance. I have no hesitation in saying that this is a serious mistake, because feedback should also highlight positive aspects.

Focusing only on what is not going well is not a sign of caring. As your team members also need reassurance about what they are doing right, the absence of positive feedback is easily interpreted as a lack of interest, appreciation, and recognition. How can you expect your employees to stay motivated if they feel neither appreciated nor recognized? The answer is obvious.

The worst approach is what some refer to as the "sandwich method." According to this theory, before addressing negative issues, you should begin with positive points. After these compliments, you can finally deliver the "missile." To make the "missile" easier to swallow, you finish with more positive remarks. This "coating" is supposed to lessen the pain for the "victim." However, this recipe—or rather, this form of anesthesia—is usually quickly seen through by employees, who recognize the manipulative nature of the tactic. After a few instances, a Pavlovian reflex sets in: as soon as the first compliment is given, the employee braces for the "missile." Conditioned to expect criticism after any positive feedback, they eventually become unable to appreciate genuine praise that is not followed by a negative comment.

One common trait of the "sandwich" approach is that positive points are presented first, only to be followed by a "but"—a coordinating conjunction used detrimentally. As it tends to negate what was said earlier (for example: "you work quickly but... poorly"), this conjunction should be avoided in caring feedback. The pattern is so obvious that the sandwich technique, when it includes a "but," is often colloquially called the "butt sandwich" (a play on the conjunction "but").

In Practice

To avoid this conditioning and maintain a climate of mutual trust, it is imperative to regularly provide feedback, whether positive or negative: when a behavior is good, acknowledge it. This will reinforce the behavior concerned. Conversely, when a behavior needs to be modified, express it just as directly, but always with caring.

Thanks to your honesty, your employees will always know what you think. Being "straightforward" does not prevent being caring but at least has the merit of maintaining a climate of sincerity, without manipulative artifice. Caring is transmitted differently than through rhetorical devices such as the "butt sandwich" and even less through complacency (which is often a manifestation of cowardice). When your employees know that you express what you really think, they naturally feel safer than if they have to read between the lines.

The overall perception that employees have of their leader's credibility always considers the perception of their caring, sincerity, and courage. It also depends on how they give feedback. As a result, giving and receiving feedback is far from just a routine exercise.

Effective feedback has its rules, and here too, it is highly recommended that the team discusses them for inclusion in their charter. These rules should, for example, take into account cultural differences: you cannot give feedback to an Asian colleague in the same way that you would to a Swiss or an American colleague. It is easy to imagine the difficulty in communicating within a multicultural team that brings together Germans, South Americans, Scandinavians, Chinese, and Indians. Discussing these cultural differences and agreeing on a modus vivendi will mitigate the difficulty in giving feedback. The debate within the framework of developing the charter also helps to clarify the spirit of caring feedback and its place in team hygiene to achieve a true feedback culture.

Here are some keys for fair and caring feedback.

1. **Giving feedback**

   - As giving feedback to someone who is not receptive is like talking to a brick wall, make sure that the recipient is receptive, for example, by asking if it is a good time for a feedback conversation.
   - For feedback to be effective, it should be given while the situation is still fresh in everyone's mind, but not in the heat of the moment. If feedback is delayed too long, its impact is diminished. As feedback can only reflect the perception of the giver, you should use "I" to express what YOU have observed. Avoid using "one," "we," or other personal pronouns that do not specify who is really expressing themselves.
   - Because you can only observe behaviors and highlight their positive or negative effects, your feedback should only address these and not the recipient personally.
   - For your feedback to be well understood, it must refer to concrete and precise examples. You should avoid generalities that are difficult to associate with situations experienced by the recipient.
   - The goal being to help the recipient, your feedback must be constructive and accompanied, if possible, by suggestions for improvement.
   - To help the recipient to digest your message, you should address only one behavior per feedback discussion. The situation may be different during a group caring feedback session.

2. **Receiving feedback**

   - You should prepare to receive caring feedback in a constructive way. Recognize that giving feedback is not easy and that it is offered for your benefit. Try to make the process as smooth as possible for the person making the effort to provide it. Therefore, refrain from arguing or trying to justify yourself.
   - To make the most of it, ensure that you understand both the concrete examples and the consequences of the behavior discussed in the feedback.
   - As feedback from the giver reflects only their personal perspective, it is in your best interest to check with other observers to see if they share the same perception.
   - Because the purpose of feedback is to help you grow, remember that it is a gift—so be sure to thank the person who gave it to you.

Lever 51 • Ensure Psychological Safety and Maintain a Positive Culture (without Fear)

As extensively developed above, employee fear is a sign of dysfunction. It may, for example, be due to:

- A management that uses force or threats to achieve its goals and, therefore, is no longer trustworthy. To impose is to constrain.
- The exercise of power without counter-power, which opens the door to abuse of power and loss of trust.
- Rules not being respected, or the absence of a system protecting those who respect them, which makes them insecure.
- Lack of trust in the institution or its leaders.

It goes without saying that fear is always present when people no longer trust institutions or leaders to protect them. As soon as they know that they are at someone's mercy, they can only live in fear.

Because the essence of leadership rests on employees' trust in their leader (see Chap. 2), the feeling of fear testifies to failing leadership.

In Practice

The antidote at the governance level is to ensure that the culture is positive and free from fear. This is your job!

To determine if this is the case, it is sufficient, for example, to ask employees, under conditions of anonymity that sufficiently protect them to answer honestly, to what extent they fear expressing openly what they think. This indicator helps to measure the level of psychological safety—or, conversely, the presence of fear—much like pain levels are measured in hospitals. Although this measure remains highly subjective, its lack of precision does not detract from the value of the information obtained.

Measuring the feeling of fear is also a very good way of verifying if employees have responded sincerely to the basic question "Who wants to be led by me?" (see Lever 24). If they are afraid, they will likely not tell the truth unless they know that they are safe from reprisals.

As it is also an indirect way of measuring the level of trust, measuring the feeling of fear[25] **should therefore serve as a hygiene indicator for all teams.**

---

[25] www.EazyMirror.com can easily be used to create a customized survey.

Even the Dog Fears Nothing...

One day, an old African dog goes butterfly hunting and realizes he is lost. Wandering aimlessly trying to find his way, he sees a young leopard running toward him with the clear intention of making a good meal.

The old dog thinks: "Oh, oh! I'm really in trouble here!"

Noticing a few bones from a carcass lying on the ground nearby, he immediately begins to chew on the bones, turning his back to the approaching leopard.

When the leopard is about to pounce on him, the old dog exclaims loudly: "Yeah, that leopard was excellent! I wonder if there are others around here?"

Hearing this, the young leopard interrupts his attack in mid-leap, looks at the dog with fright, and flees, crawling under the bushes.

"Whew!" sighs the leopard, "that was close. That old dog almost got me!"

However, a monkey, who had observed the whole scene from a nearby tree branch, thinks that he can profit from what he knows by negotiating with the leopard and thus obtaining his protection. So he goes after him, but the old dog, seeing him running at full speed after the leopard, realizes that something must be brewing. The monkey catches up with the leopard, reveals the trick, and proposes a deal.

The young leopard is furious at having been deceived: "Come here monkey, get on my back, and you'll see what happens to that clever one!"

The old dog sees the leopard rushing with the monkey on his back and worries: "What am I going to do now?"

But instead of fleeing, the dog sits with his back to his aggressors, once again pretending not to have seen them, and just as they come within earshot, he exclaims: "Where is that damn monkey? I sent him an hour ago to find me another leopard!"

A good antidote to fear is building a positive culture. This culture should advocate an optimistic approach to life based on positive psychology,[26] as promoted by Professor Emeritus Philippe Gabillet. Encourage your employees to focus on the glass half full rather than the glass half empty.[27] They will develop a more favorable and energizing vision.

An even better antidote is to deploy the engagement model (see Fig. 2.2 in Chap. 2). This model is based on the PFC framework: performance, fairness, and caring (see Fig. 2.1). When fairness and caring are practiced, they create psychological safety. When there is psychological safety, there is no room for abuse of power. When there is no room for abuse of power, employees have no reason to be fearful. When there is no fear, you create a virtuous circle (see Fig. 5.2).

---

[26] https://en.wikipedia.org/wiki/Positive_psychology

[27] For information, engineers have ended the debate about whether the glass is half full or half empty by simply considering that the glass was just oversized...

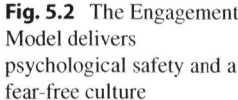

Fig. 5.2 The Engagement
Model delivers
psychological safety and a
fear-free culture

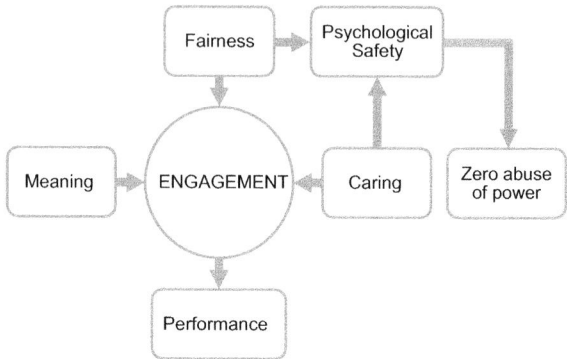

As indicated in Chap. 2, the feeling of psychological safety is at the heart of the book "Care to Dare: Unleashing Astonishing Potential Through Secure Base Leadership,"[28] whose content complements, in many ways, some of the levers presented in this work. It advocates, as I do, the necessity of ensuring that employees feel safe. Without this, no trust is possible.

To build trust, it is essential to attribute positive intentions to employees. When you do the opposite and attribute negative intentions to others, you automatically establish a relationship based on mistrust and the search for scapegoats. You will not develop trust by looking for someone to blame.

Testimonial of Indra Nooyi, CEO of PepsiCo
The message of Indra Nooyi, CEO of PepsiCo, presents an excellent example of acceptance and positive reinforcement:

"My father was an absolutely wonderful human being. From him I learned to always assume positive intent. Whatever anybody says or does, assume positive intent. You will be amazed at how your whole approach to a person or problem becomes very different. When you assume negative intent, you're angry. If you take away that anger and assume positive intent, you will be amazed. Your emotional quotient goes up because you are no longer almost random in your response. You don't get defensive. You don't scream. You are trying to understand and listen because at your basic core you are saying, "Maybe they are saying something to me that I'm not hearing." So "assume positive intent" has been a huge piece of advice for me.

In business, sometimes in the heat of the moment, people say things. You can either misconstrue what they're saying and assume they are trying to put you down, or you can say, 'Wait a minute. Let me really get behind what they are saying to understand whether they're reacting because they're hurt, upset,

---

[28] George Kohlrieser, Susan Goldsworthy, and Duncan Coombe, op. cit.

confused, or they don't understand what it is I've asked them to do.' If you react from a negative perspective—because you didn't like the way they reacted—then it just becomes two negatives fighting each other. But when you assume positive intent, I think often what happens is the other person says, 'Hey, wait a minute, maybe I'm wrong in reacting the way I do because this person is really making an effort.'"[29]

Lever 52 • Zero Tolerance for Malevolence, Ill Will, and Bad Faith

The "No Asshole Rule" may seem excessive to some. They might think that such individuals are inevitable and must be tolerated. I do not share this view, but I wish the best of luck to those who are willing to welcome and keep assholes in their organizations.

To take the reasoning to its logical conclusion, I recommend complementing the "No Asshole Rule" by adding "zero tolerance for malevolence." The "No Asshole Rule" results in getting rid of... "assholes, " whereas "zero malevolence" goes even further: even in the absence of assholes, you prohibit and sanction all acts of malevolence, even occasional ones. Indeed, one can be malevolent without being an asshole. Malevolence is sadly not reserved only for assholes...

Those who frequently practice malevolence are very likely to become assholes, especially if they are not stopped early. Zero tolerance for malevolence is specifically meant to prevent malevolent people from:

- Becoming assholes
- Believing that, in the absence of sanctions, it is acceptable to be malevolent

In short, zero tolerance for malevolence is the vaccine against assholes!

You might wonder why not limit yourselves to "zero tolerance for malevolence" without adding the "No Asshole Rule." The answer is that the latter allows you to tell assholes that they have no place in the organization and then to remove those who may have slipped through the cracks of zero tolerance for malevolence. It is therefore the means of getting rid of historical assholes, those who have survived under the old, more lax rules.

I have extended this prohibition to include ill will because the latter is the antithesis of engagement. Any person, manager, or employee, who is resistant or who does not invest themselves acts as a hurdle that sabotages collective success. To the extent that ill will harms the organization, some might argue that it is already a form of malevolence. However, I recognize that depending on the circumstances it

---

[29] Cecily D. Cooper, Don Hellriegel, and John W. Slocum Jr. "Mastering Organizational Behavior Version 14.0", Flat World Knowledge, 2017.

may not always be malevolent.[30] I am willing to risk some repetition to ensure that nothing is overlooked.

Lever 53 • Promote Diversity and Inclusion

The absence of discrimination automatically results from implementing fair and caring leadership, but this does not necessarily mean that "others," those who are different, are encouraged to join the organization. There is indeed a difference between not discriminating and truly accepting.

Caring governance should include a proactive approach to promoting diversity. The way we welcome others expresses our level of openness of heart and mind, so this question could have been listed as a character trait (in the framework of "Complete Framework for Building Trust, High Engagement, and High Performance" at end of this book) or even as an expected behavior (in the following column). However, I deliberately placed it in the column for framework conditions that address governance, because it concerns not only the leader but everyone in the organization.

In Practice

Making life easier for parents of young children (daycare, schedules, etc.) is one aspect of diversity: by allowing them to organize themselves, you accept that they have constraints different from those who do not have, or no longer have, young children. The same applies to religious diversity or gender diversity. Implementing arrangements that allow everyone to function in harmony with their characteristics is obviously caring insofar as it does not compromise the imperative of sustainability and performance.

A blatant example is organizations' resistance to accepting job sharing. It is almost always a refusal, in principle, motivated only by preconceptions about the difficulty of this mode of operation. Having tested it successfully, I can affirm that it is not only possible but also offers significant advantages for both parties. The employee who does not want to work full-time can find a more interesting job that they would not have had access to otherwise. The employer has access to talents who are unable to work full-time while having a team that manages to get the work done, regardless of vacations, illnesses, and other problems that can create challenges for a manager without reliable backup. The model has its difficulties, but they are not more insurmountable than those of a more traditional approach.

Managing intercultural differences is another dimension to consider in this context. It would be unkind to impose a single mode of operation on employees from different cultures. The hope of erasing cultural differences by assuming that everyone will fit into the one-size-fits-all mold of corporate culture is an illusion

---

[30] It can happen that people show ill will, not out of malevolence, but simply because they do not support the project for one reason or another.

that lulls many leaders. The reality is much more prosaic: people pretend, but without really feeling comfortable. The more they pretend, the less engaged they become, and the more misunderstandings arise.

A healthy consideration of cultural differences is a necessity, even if it is far from easy. The debate around the Engaged Team Charter is a very good forum for confronting cultural differences and agreeing on how to manage them (expected behaviors, governance rules...) within this team.

Welcoming differences with open arms means accepting to take into account the needs of others with care. As considering the interests of others is at the center of caring, implementing governance that promotes diversity and inclusion appears unavoidable to me.

5.4   Visual Summary: Fair and Caring Leadership Operating Framework

Figure 5.3 provides a visual summary of the Fair and Caring Leadership levers for the operating framework

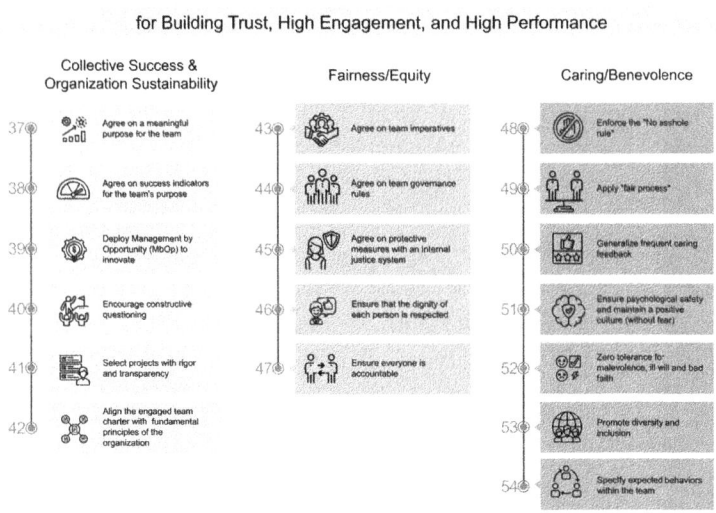

Fig. 5.3   Summary of the levers for the operating Framework for a Fair and Caring Leadership

Epilogue

THE Main Concern

Before concluding, I would like to remind you of the necessity to relentlessly ask yourself the eight key leadership questions[1] when interacting with your teams. As they put their finger on what is essential, they should, in my opinion, be an ever-present concern. Systematically asking them before any statement, decision, or action should become a reflex for you. As they all revolve around the main levers of engagement, keeping them in mind can serve as a valuable mental guide.

These questions stem from everything that has been said previously. Apart from the first one, which is unavoidable, the order of the next six is not important because the answer to each of these questions contributes to the ultimate result expressed by the first. It will, of course, be up to you to use your judgment to correctly anticipate the answers that they call for. Poor anticipation will demonstrate an error in judgment that will impact the level of engagement and therefore performance.

Because not saying/deciding/doing is also taken into account by your employees, you must ask these questions even when you refrain from saying/deciding/doing.

Sort It Out

After this overview of the many levers that support your teams' engagement, I return to the starting point announced in Chaps. 2 and 3: Without trust, no engaged followers!

I therefore invite you to review the summary table presented in "Complete Framework for Building Trust, High Engagement, and High Performance" and ask yourself the following question: among all the levers mentioned in this table, which ones can be removed without their absence reducing the level of trust and therefore engagement of your employees? Depending on the environments, there may indeed be a few that are not relevant. Cross them out without hesitation!

Even if, out of the fifty or so levers proposed, you have crossed out a few, there should still be several that are worth considering in order to become—or

---

[1] Lever 6.

© The Editor(s) (if applicable) and The Author(s), under exclusive license to
Springer Nature Switzerland AG 2026
R. H Cohen, *Driving Employee Engagement*, Management for Professionals,
https://doi.org/10.1007/978-3-032-05172-1

remain—trustworthy. By evaluating your level of performance on each of these levers, you will be able to get an idea of your ability to generate engagement as well as identify the potential benefits of improving some of these levers. Reminder: To allow you to self-evaluate, the summary table can be downloaded at www.driving-engagement.com/download. It contains a column in which you can enter your score for each lever on a scale of 0–4.

I hope, however, that by noting that there are many levers that deserve your attention, you will not fall into the easy solution of throwing in the towel by saying that it is impossible. Even if it is manifestly difficult, it is not out of reach. I have met enough fair and caring leaders to affirm that it is entirely feasible. The few authentic testimonials included in this book should dispel any doubt about its feasibility. This does not mean that it is within everyone's reach. Just as not everyone is meant to be an athlete, math teacher, artist, or engineer, not everyone is meant to be a leader. It is up to each person to be clear sighted about the role that suits them or not.

One of my objectives was, with an approach as holistic as possible, to highlight the complexity of the task as well as the links or interdependencies between all the levers that influence trust in the leader.

The other objective, arguably the most important, was to encourage you to take a step back and reflect on what it truly means to be a leader. My hope is that, through this reflection, some of you have discovered insights that will help you to enhance not only your own satisfaction as a leader but also the job satisfaction of your employees.

Caution: Identifying the keys is valuable but putting them into practice is even better. It is up to you to become ambassadors of fair and caring leadership, showing that it can be practiced every day. As I have your success at heart, do not hesitate to send me your testimonials to contribute to the next edition of this book.

Complete Framework for Building Trust, High Engagement, and High Performance

The comprehensive Fair and Caring Leadership Framework, encompassing all levers for building trust, high engagement, and high performance, is presented in Fig. 1 (divided into three components owing to space constraints: 1a focusing on performance foundations, 1b detailing fairness mechanisms, and 1c outlining caring practices).

This framework is visually structured around three interconnected imperatives—performance, fairness, and caring—each forming a horizontal axis (each one is shown in one of the three components of Fig. 1).

Framework for Building Trust, High Engagement, and High Performance

Imperatives of Fair and Caring Leadership	Lever	Your Fair and Caring Leadership behaviors	Lever	Your Fair and Caring Leadership traits	Lever	Your Fair and Caring Leadership operating framework that fosters engagement
	1	SMART is not enough: provide corresponding resources and information	19	Be a source of inspiration	37	Agree on a meaningful purpose for the team
	2	Make your expectations explicit	20	Maintain your credibility daily	38	Agree on success indicators for the team's purpose
Collective Success & Organization Sustainability	3	Trust them	21	Cultivate your resilience	39	Deploy Management by Opportunity (MbOp) to innovate
	4	Share information and knowledge	22	Share your passion with your employees	40	Encourage constructive questioning
	5	Attract and develop talents	23	Be genuinely authentic	41	Select projects with rigor and transparency
	6	Ask yourself the leader's eight questions	24	Have engaged followers	42	Align the engaged team charter with fundamental principles of the organization

(a) Performance-Focused Levers of Fair and Caring Leadership Framework

Fig. 1 Recap of the levers constituting the complete framework for Building Trust, High Engagement, and High Performance, divided into three subtables

R. H Cohen, *Driving Employee Engagement*, Management for Professionals, https://doi.org/10.1007/978-3-032-05172-1

Framework for Building Trust, High Engagement, and High Performance

Imperatives of Fair and Caring Leadership	Lever	Your Fair and Caring Leadership behaviors	Lever	Your Fair and Caring Leadership traits	Lever	Your Fair and Caring Leadership operating framework that fosters engagement
	7	Walk the talk	25	Demonstrate fairness	43	Agree on team imperatives
	8	Balance the four fundamental interests (personal, employer, employees, civil society)	26	Demonstrate rigor	44	Agree on team governance rules
Fairness/ Equity	9	Ensure the safety and well-being of your employees	27	Be courageous	45	Agree on protective measures with an internal justice system
	10	Renounce paradoxical injunctions	28	Ensure congruence and coherence	46	Ensure that the dignity of each person is respected
	11	Recognize everyone's contribution and reward those who deserve it	29	Demonstrate wisdom / discernment	47	Ensure that everyone is accountable

(b) Fairness-Focused Levers of Fair and Caring Leadership Framework

Framework for Building Trust, High Engagement, and High Performance

Imperatives of Fair and Caring Leadership	Lever	Your Fair and Caring Leadership behaviors	Lever	Your Fair and Caring Leadership traits	Lever	Your Fair and Caring Leadership operating framework that fosters engagement
	12	Empower people	30	Demonstrate humanity	48	Enforce the "No asshole rule"
	13	Boost your employees' resilience and self-confidence	31	Develop your emotional intelligence	49	Apply "fair process"
	14	Support your employees and make yourself available	32	Be humble and vulnerable	50	Generalize frequent caring feedback
Caring/ Benevolence	15	Develop your employees' employability	33	Know yourself without self-deception	51	Ensure psychological safety and maintain a positive culture (without fear)
	16	Capitalize on your employees' strengths	34	No cowardice	52	Zero tolerance for malevolence, ill will and bad faith
	17	Prevent demotivation of your employees	35	Find sources of gratification and joy in interaction and leadership	53	Promote diversity and inclusion
	18	No corporate double-speak	36	Act in a caring way	54	Specify expected behaviors within the team

(c) Caring-Focused Levers of Fair and Caring Leadership Framework

Fig. 1 (continued)

For each imperative, the framework details vertically **18 behaviors, 18 personality traits, and 18 governance conditions**, collectively constituting the 54 levers of Fair and Caring Leadership.

These levers are not isolated; rather, they interact and reinforce one another, reflecting the complex reality of leadership in today's organizations.

The complexity of leadership makes it impossible to propose a one-size-fits-all formula. The intent of this framework is therefore to offer leaders a comprehensive set of ingredients from which to craft their own approach. Each leader, team, and organization is unique, and the optimal "recipe" will vary depending on context, personality, culture, and evolving needs. The framework encourages leaders to reflect on which levers are most relevant to their situation and to experiment with different combinations and intensities.

The only reliable way of assessing whether the chosen approach is effective is by measuring the resulting levels of engagement and trust within the team.

To support this process, the framework is designed as both a diagnostic and a developmental tool. Leaders are encouraged to use the downloadable version of this framework from www.driving-engagement.com/download to regularly assess their strengths and areas for improvement across all 54 levers. This self-assessment can be done individually or as a team exercise, fostering open dialogue about what is working well and where there is room for growth. By making this reflection a regular practice, leaders can ensure that their approach remains dynamic and responsive to changing circumstances.

Integrating the levers into daily leadership practice requires intentionality and persistence. It is not enough to simply be aware of the framework; the real impact comes from translating these principles into concrete actions, decisions, and interactions. Leaders should look for opportunities to reinforce performance, fairness, and caring in everyday moments—whether through feedback, recognition, decision making, or conflict resolution.

Finally, the framework serves as a reminder that leadership is a journey, not a destination. Mastery is not about perfection but about continuous learning, adaptation, and self-awareness. By embracing the holistic approach of Fair and Caring Leadership, leaders can create resilient, inclusive environments where trust is sustained, engagement is maximized, and collective success becomes a lasting reality.

GPSR Compliance

The European Union's (EU) General Product Safety Regulation (GPSR) is a set of rules that requires consumer products to be safe and our obligations to ensure this.

If you have any concerns about our products, you can contact us on ProductSafety@springernature.com

In case Publisher is established outside the EU, the EU authorized representative is:

Springer Nature Customer Service Center GmbH
Europaplatz 3
69115 Heidelberg, Germany

Batch number: 10130287

Printed by Printforce, the Netherlands